A Guide for
Planning and Implementing
Instruction for Adults

JOHN M. DIRKX
SUZANNE M. PRENGER

A Guide
for Planning and
Implementing
Instruction
for Adults

A Theme-Based Approach

JOSSEY-BASS PUBLISHERS ▪ San Francisco

Substantial discounts on bulk quantities of Jossey-Bass books are available to corporations, professional associations, and other organizations. For details and discount information, contact the special sales department at Jossey-Bass Inc., Publishers (415) 433–1740; Fax (800) 605–2665.

For sales outside the United States, please contact your local Simon & Schuster International office.

Jossey-Bass Web address: http://www.josseybass.com

Manufactured in the United States of America

Library of Congress Cataloging-in-Publication Data
Dirkx, John M., date.
   A guide for planning and implementing instruction for adults: a theme-based approach / John M. Dirkx, Suzanne M. Prenger. — 1st ed.
      p.   cm. — (The Jossey-Bass higher and adult education series)
   Includes bibliographical references and index.
   ISBN 0–7879–0837–1 (cloth: acid-free paper)
   1. Adult education—United States. 2. Functional literacy—United States. 3. Unit method of teaching. 4. Curriculum planning—United States. I. Prenger, Suzanne M., date. II. Title. III. Series.
LC5251.D56 1997
373'.012—dc21   96–51281

FIRST EDITION
PB Printing   10 9 8 7 6 5 4 3 2 1

The Jossey-Bass
Higher and Adult Education Series

CONTENTS

PREFACE

The purpose of *A Guide for Planning and Implementing Instruction for Adults: A Theme-Based Approach* is to help teachers plan and implement integrated, theme-based (ITB) instruction for adults. Programs and learning settings within the intended scope of this guidebook include but are not limited to adult literacy, basic and secondary (GED) education, English as a Second Language (ESL), family literacy programs such as Even Start and Head Start, and workplace education. For purposes of the *Guide*, we will refer to these programs as developmental education.

Because of the diverse settings of these programs and the communities they are intended to serve, it is difficult to generalize about their learners in any meaningful manner. Regardless of their background, educational achievement, or specific goals, however, individuals in these programs are all seeking to improve their knowledge and skills related to the particular contexts in which they find themselves. These skills may range from learning to read and write their own names to communicating in English to developing problem-solving, critical thinking, and lifelong learning skills within their jobs, families, or communities. While some are learning to obtain a job that will enable them to get or stay off welfare, others are hoping to brush up on academic skills so that they can be admitted into postsecondary educational institutions. Still others simply want to be able to read to their children or grandchildren. Women and men of all ages, employed, underemployed, and unemployed, from diverse cultural backgrounds and countries all over the world, enter these educational programs to pursue a variety of goals. The one thing they have in common is the relationship of their life contexts as adults to their participation in adult learning and what they want or need to learn. This relationship is the basis for an ITB approach to instruction and is a central assumption of this book.

Why Consider an ITB Approach to Instruction?

Student persistence and completion represents one of the most difficult problems that adult developmental education programs face. A small proportion of learners in these programs are highly motivated to accomplish their objectives and move on to other things. A majority of students in many of these programs, however, either do not complete their educational goals or start and stop repeatedly, sometimes taking years to complete a program of study that could easily be accomplished in a year or less of persistent study. While many factors have been identified as possible reasons for these difficulties, recent studies show that persistence and attendance is clearly associated with characteristics of the program, especially the nature of the curriculum. That is, what is learned and how it is learned are factors influencing a student's motivation to continue.

Within many adult developmental education settings, typical approaches to teaching and learning place mastery of academic knowledge and skills at the center of the instructional process. Traditional strategies, grounded in the principles of instructional design, assess learners' needs within this focus. Methods and materials are then selected that seem most relevant or appropriate to meeting these needs. Each of the subject areas tends to be taught in discrete units, separate from each other and from the learners' experiences. Their life contexts, if they are considered at all, serve as a kind of psychological backdrop to the principal work of mastering predetermined academic skills and knowledge.

Literacy educators have long recognized that relating instructional content to the specific contexts of learners' lives and interests increases motivation to learn. Recently, in adult basic and literacy education, there has been increased emphasis on grounding curriculum and instruction more thoroughly in learners' concrete life contexts. This emphasis on *contextual* learning (Auerbach, 1989; Rogoff & Lave, 1984; Sticht, 1991) also helps learners persist in relatively long commitments to their educational program (Fingeret, 1990). Recognizing the importance of the learners' experiences to the learning process, this approach stands in sharp contrast to the subject matter–focused and workbook-based approach that dominates more traditional instructional strategies. Using bus schedules and newspapers to teach reading skills, balancing a checkbook and determining a household budget to teach math skills, and writing letters for job applications are examples of these "life context" methods. Examples of these programmatic approaches include family and intergenerational literacy and workplace basic skills. These approaches reflect an emphasis on integrating traditional academic skills and content with the life contexts of the adult learners. Such an emphasis can have dramatic effects on student persistence and attendance.

Yet, even so-called life skills approaches often focus primarily on mastery of academic skills and competencies, using the different situations as ways to "contextualize" material. Here, too, the different subjects are often taught as discrete topics or bodies of knowledge (Brady, 1989). For example, math is often taught through the applications of specific life contexts in which calculation is used or needed. Adults are encouraged to use manuals from work or books they want to read to their children as resources for learning to read more effectively. Writing letters and filling out job applications are viewed as means of improving adults' writing abilities. The focus remains on the specific academic subject, which continues to structure and guide the instructional process, and life contexts are treated as resources to facilitate learning within these specific areas.

Rather than marginalizing life contexts as instructional resources, or ignoring them altogether, the approach described in this *Guide* places the learner's life contexts at the center of the instructional process. Instruction is structured around a theme that captures the relevant experiences, interests, and needs of the adult learner. Themes such as "getting a job," "raising my child safely," or "dealing with absentee landlords" represent ways of thinking about knowledge that are quite different from the traditional academic units, such as math, reading, or writing, which structure most developmental programs for adults.

Themes provide a basis for integrating these traditional domains of academic competence with particular issues or concerns that are directly relevant and meaningful to the learners' life contexts. Rather than being taught as discrete subjects, these different domains are integrated with each other and with the particular life context that the instructional theme represents. Integrated, thematic approaches to instruction deepen the learners' understanding of the theme they are studying, while also promoting mastery of basic skills and facilitating development of other process skills, such as problem solving, critical thinking, learning-to-learn, teamwork, and other interpersonal communication skills. Traditional or life skills approaches often tend to focus on unidimensional strategies for learning. That is, a unit designed to teach writing focuses primarily on the specific objectives and competencies intended within the unit. Integrated, thematic approaches, however, are multilayered. Any given instructional experience represents an opportunity to learn a number of things. In the words of one instructor, integrated approaches to instruction are like "peeling back the layers of an onion."

Integrated, thematic approaches are also more responsive to individual and group needs as they arise within the context of the instructional process. Traditional approaches to instructing adults rely on determining objectives and content before the educational experience begins. Integrated, thematic approaches, however, use topics as general ways to organize the instructional process. More specific instructional objectives and relevant content emerge from the educational experience itself. For example, helping a fellow student handle problems with her roommate allows a learner to better understand the things that are meaningful and important within his life.

Many teachers of adults, adhering to traditional approaches to instruction, view the manifestation of psychosocial content within the teaching and learning setting as "baggage" that learners inevitably bring with them. Teachers understand that it is necessary to provide learners with some time to "vent" their feelings and get things "off their chests"; teachers see such venting as a "prerequisite" to learning, but not as an integral part of it. In integrated thematic approaches, this psychosocial "baggage" becomes the very context for learning. Rather than seeing it as split off from real learning, teachers see it as necessary to a personally significant and meaningful kind of learning.

Need for the *Guide*

Practitioners who want to shift toward a more contextual approach to curriculum and instruction find that such a move requires some rethinking of what they do and of their relationships with their learners. Given that most practitioners in adult developmental education programs work elsewhere, are part-time, and are already strapped for time and resources, the tasks involved in this approach present significant challenges. Program directors and instructors in adult developmental education programs have trouble obtaining guidance in how to integrate academic competencies and other important skills successfully into learners' life contexts.

In North America, there have been some attempts to describe the ITB approach applied at the basic skills levels to pre-GED and GED preparation (Ministry of Advanced Education and Job Training, 1987; Soifer et al., 1990). In general, however, these prior efforts only illustrate how contextual or theme-based instruction can be applied to GED preparation, and they often rely on traditional curricular content. Theme-based materials and programs that are currently available target adults learning basic skills specific to performing job tasks. Publishers have attempted to incorporate more contextually relevant and meaningful content into basic skills materials (e.g., recent promotional material on GED preparation from Cambridge, The Adult Education Company offers "new up-to-date content with life-skills relevance" and "pre-reading prompts" that "relate content to the students' prior knowledge and life-skills concerns"). The effectiveness of these materials in helping learners connect the content of their learning with their own contexts and experiences remains largely untested, however.

To be sure we were not missing exemplar projects or materials not reported in the literature, we telephoned several individuals in key positions of information dissemination in the field of adult basic and literacy education. These contacts could not identify any guides, handbooks, or materials related to curriculum development for GED preparation or other descriptions of curriculum development that used an ITB approach.

After this survey, we became aware of a project being conducted by the Adult Basic Literacy Educators (ABLE) Network in Seattle, Washington. The ABLE network produced a manual titled *I*CANS: Integrated Curriculum for Achieving Necessary Skills* (Adult Basic Literacy Educators Network, n.d.). This manual is both similar to and different from the present *Guide*. While the *I*CANS* manual seeks to foster an integrated, thematic approach to curriculum and instruction, it is structured largely around the Secretary's Commission on Achieving Necessary Skills, or SCANS (1991), competencies. The purpose of our *Guide* is to build on the ideas presented in the *I*CANS* manual and to present a more holistic and comprehensive approach to integrated, thematic instruction. We are indebted to the staff of the ABLE Network for their willingness to cooperate with the writing of this *Guide* and their permission to use the many good ideas they have developed.

The absence of an effective, written, and accessible curriculum guide and handbook for ITB approaches to adult basic education (ABE) or the GED is not surprising. Individuals who may be effectively providing instruction in an integrated manner are, for the most part, instructors who have barely any additional time to reflect on and document what they do. If and when integration of academic competencies with life contexts occurs in developmental education, it appears to be largely ad hoc and intuitive. One instructor reported that, although she has been using an ITB approach for several years, she had not thought about the process she used for doing this. Two instructors associated with Even Start strongly endorsed the concept of an ITB approach for basic skills and GED preparation, but pointed out the need for a written curriculum guide. For the most part, developmental curricula continue to be primarily subject- or discipline-based and driven directly by the specific competencies being evaluated through testing or job performance. Clearly, there is a strong need for a guidebook on planning and implementing integrated, thematic instruction in adult developmental education.

How We Developed the *Guide*

The present *Guide* emerged from a project we conducted to develop a manual teachers could use to plan and implement ITB instruction. In doing this project, we intended to deepen our understanding of the theoretical basis for an integrated, thematic approach in adult education, to identify the implicit theories and beliefs that guide the work of selected teachers using this approach, and to study the implementation of the approach within various settings of adult learning. The *Guide* represents our synthesis of the research and theory on integrated, thematic approaches to instruction and our analysis of what practitioners who use these approaches say and do within developmental education settings.

Thus, we developed this *Guide* with the goal of making explicit the assumptions, knowledge, strategies, resources, and processes that instructors are using to integrate their curricula. We selected instructors of adults who worked within the United States in different kinds of educational programs and who were known for their use of integrated and thematic approaches to instruction. These programs included adult basic and secondary education, ESL, and workplace and family literacy programs. The instructors were identified through our discussions with administrators, directors, curriculum developers, and teachers. After the instructors were identified, we called them to explain the project and to ask them to describe their approach to instruction. Based on these informal, preliminary interviews and our desire to represent a variety of instructional programs within the project, we selected several teachers in Nebraska, Oregon, and New York. We traveled to their sites to observe their instruction and to conduct in-depth interviews about their teaching. Observations of the learning settings were videotaped, and all interviews with teachers were audiotaped and transcribed. Using qualitative methods, we then analyzed the observations and interviews to determine how the participating instructors understood, interpreted, and implemented integrated or thematic instruction.

Several instructors in adult developmental education programs reviewed earlier versions of the *Guide.* In addition, summaries of the *Guide* have been presented at several state, regional, and national conferences on the instruction of adults. We have incorporated critiques from the instructors and conference participants into the final revisions of the book. Many of the specific strategies and techniques discussed in this *Guide* represent ideas that the teachers provided, and we acknowledge our debt to them whenever possible.

An Overview of the *Guide* and How to Use It

The following chapters and sections of this *Guide* provide more specific information on the use of an integrated approach to GED preparation. Chapter One provides an overview of integrated, thematic instruction. Chapter Two discusses important assumptions about how adults learn. Chapter Three provides a general discussion of differences among individuals in their approach to learning, and context-based instruction and processes to use in implementing this approach to ABE/GED preparation. The purpose of Chapter Three is to provide a conceptual framework in which you can organize your instructional planning and decision making. Chapter Four describes specific processes to use in selecting and planning theme units, including strategies you can use to identify themes. Chapter Five contains several sample theme units that are intended to illustrate how you might plan and organize units around particular learner themes. Chapter Five is for illustrative purposes only. We think these sample theme units can help you start a theme-based approach, but we certainly do not intend them to be prescriptive or exhaustive. Chapter Six provides a more detailed description of specific instructional strategies that you may find helpful in implementing a thematic approach to instruction. Chapter Seven provides an overview to assessing instruction and student learning within this approach. Chapter Seven also lists resource materials that you may want to peruse. Chapter Eight discusses ways to meet the challenges of ITB instruction. Finally, the three Resources provide information to help further develop your understanding of and approach to ITB instruction.

The emphasis here is on "guide." A recipe-like, how-to book or manual is neither a desirable nor an appropriate tool to help adult educators implement ITB instruction. Such a manual would violate many of the basic premises of this approach to adult education and, indeed, several of the general principles of adult education. We are confident, however, that practitioners at all levels will benefit from practical suggestions and advice as to what this form of education involves and how one might go about using it.

The present text is written in the form of a guide or handbook, rather than a specific curriculum or step-by-step manual. *A Guide for Planning and Implementing Instruction for Adults* helps program directors and instructors integrate academic competencies with themes that are relevant to the experiences and life contexts of their adult learners. The *Guide* will be particularly helpful to educators seeking to enhance employment, family, and other life skills orientations within their educational programs. We intend for you to consult the *Guide* from time to time, perhaps more often at first until you become experienced with this approach.

February 1997

John M. Dirkx
East Lansing, Michigan

Suzanne M. Prenger
Lincoln, Nebraska

ACKNOWLEDGMENTS

Many people helped us develop *A Guide for Planning and Implementing Instruction for Adults*. We especially want to thank the teachers and students who so graciously let us into their classrooms and lives in an effort to help us better understand the meaning of an ITB approach in practice. We have a special debt of gratitude to our teacher-reviewers, who provided us with invaluable feedback on drafts of this text. The clerical staff from the Nebraska Institute for the Study of Adult Literacy, including Michelle, Amy, Tona, and Wendy, was superb in helping us move this book through to completion. The computer skills of Cindy Blodgett-McDeavitt deserve special recognition. We also received much valuable advice and information from professional colleagues, too numerous to mention, throughout the United States. We thank them for their interest in and support of this project. The editorial staff at Jossey-Bass has been enormously helpful, and we appreciate their assistance and patience.

In the early stages of our project, many people were very helpful in pointing us toward people and programs using integrated approaches. We especially want to thank Jean Lowe at the GED testing service in Washington, D.C., the personnel at the Adult Literacy Clearinghouse in the U.S. Department of Education, Susan Imel at ERIC, Bonnie Freeman at the National Center for Family Literacy, Cheryl Harmon at the Pennsylvania Adult Education Resource Center, and instructors in Even Start programs in Salem, Oregon, and Lincoln, Nebraska.

The project that led to this *Guide* was supported in part by a grant from the Adult and Community Education Division of the Nebraska Department of Education. Additional support was provided by the Department of Vocational and Adult Education and

Teachers College at the University of Nebraska-Lincoln. Final preparation of the manuscript was supported by the Department of Educational Administration at Michigan State University.

J. M. D.
S. M. P.

THE AUTHORS

John M. Dirkx is associate professor of Higher, Adult, and Lifelong Education, and associate director of the Michigan Center for Career and Technical Education, Department of Educational Administration, Michigan State University. Prior to his present position, Dirkx was associate professor of Adult and Continuing Education at the University of Nebraska-Lincoln, and director of the Nebraska Institute for the Study of Adult Literacy, a research and development unit for adult basic and literacy education within the Department of Vocational and Adult Education. He received his bachelor's degree (1976) in medical microbiology from the University of Wisconsin-Madison. His master's (1981) and doctoral (1987) degrees in continuing and vocational education were from the University of Wisconsin-Madison.

Dirkx is coeditor of *Adult Education Quarterly* and a member of the American Association for Adult and Continuing Education, the Commission on Adult Basic Education, the Commission of Professors of Adult Education, the Academy of Human Resource Development, and the American Educational Research Association. He was named Outstanding Adult Educator for 1996 by the Association of Adult and Continuing Education of Nebraska.

Before his current work as a professor of adult and continuing education, Dirkx worked for many years as a practitioner of education for the professions, continuing education, patient education, and in-service education for public school teachers. Dirkx's research activities have focused on the dynamics of the teaching-learning relationship and experience-based learning within adult basic and literacy education and education for work. He has published articles and book chapters on the psychosocial dimensions of adult learning, group process and development, experience-based learning, student retention, staff development, and curriculum improvement. Dirkx is also coediting (with Sean Courtney) a book on teaching strategies for adult educators, and is working on a forthcoming book that focuses on discovering the self through teaching and learning.

Suzanne M. Prenger is a doctoral student in psychological and cultural studies in education at the University of Nebraska–Lincoln, where she teaches multicultural education and is project evaluator and instructor in the University Foundations for Freshmen program. She served as project coordinator for the Integrated Theme-Based Curriculum Project in the Department of Vocational and Adult Education, and cowrote curriculum for pregnant and parenting teens.

Prenger is the former academic director of the Cuernavaca, Mexico, campus of the Center for Global Education, an innovative, experiential education program for U.S. and Canadian students, faculty, and adult learners. She taught education, social policy, and human rights courses, and facilitated staff development activities in experiential and popular education. She has worked as a consultant and staff for several human rights, development, and popular education agencies in the United States and Latin America, and is a professional interpreter. She received a bachelor's degree in anthropology and Spanish from the University of Nebraska-Lincoln in 1976, conducted master's studies in Spanish and taught Spanish there until 1982, and taught the history and philosophy of education until 1984.

Her research interests include the process of transformation in the adult learner; issues of resistance in multicultural education and diversity training; law enforcement diversity training; and issues in faculty development for tenured faculty. She also continues her own education in traditional and natural medicine.

She is a member of the National Association for Multicultural Education and the North American Association of Popular and Adult Education. She is also an editorial assistant for the *Adult Education Quarterly.*

A Guide for
Planning and Implementing
Instruction for Adults

CHAPTER 1

Using Integrated, Theme-Based Instruction with Adults

The purpose of this chapter is to provide an introduction to integrated, theme-based (ITB) instruction. We will discuss (1) why ITB instruction should be used in developmental education programs for adults, (2) characteristics of an ITB perspective and how it differs from more traditional approaches, (3) a model of ITB instruction we propose in this *Guide,* and (4) tips for using the *Guide* effectively.

The Importance of ITB Instruction

The approach to instruction of adults that we describe within this *Guide* is based on an understanding of what motivates learners to persist in educational programs and how people actually learn and make sense of what they are learning. Virtually all practitioners who work with adults in developmental education programs can speak to the need to maintain and stimulate learners' motivation to persist in and complete their goals. Conventional approaches to instruction present little problem for a small proportion of highly motivated students. For example, a relatively small number of students who enroll in adult secondary education or GED programs are strongly focused on passing the GED test and getting on with their education or life goals. They will, in all likelihood, succeed in their programs, regardless of the instructional approach taken.

When you instruct these students, the best approach might simply be to provide the resources they need and to then get out of their way. A much larger proportion of students, however, simply do not stay with their programs long enough to complete this goal. They move in and out of programs for years with little evidence of educational gain or achievement (Dirkx & Jha, 1994).

Keeping adult learners sufficiently motivated and interested to complete their goals for the programs in which they are enrolled is a widespread problem (Quigley, 1992; Young, Fleischman, Fitzgerald, & Morgan, 1995). In one federally funded adult basic education program recognized nationally for its quality, for example, 67 percent of the students who enrolled within a two-year period withdrew before completing their goals. Of those students who withdrew, 46 percent had completed at least the eleventh grade in public or private schools. The average entry-level reading and math scores on the Test of Adult Base Education for students who did not continue were 9.5 and 8.2, respectively (these are grade-level equivalents). Of these students, at least 50 percent scored at the tenth-grade level or higher in reading, and at the eighth-grade level in math (Dirkx & Jha, 1994). So it is clear that many of these students bring to these educational programs achievement levels and abilities that provide a solid foundation for future growth. Yet, an overwhelming number choose to leave these instructional programs before accomplishing their goals.

Adult learners enrolled in developmental education programs, such as high school completion or workplace basic skills, face pressures and competing demands. From the perspective of federal policy, many are living in poverty or just above it. A substantial proportion of these adult learners are unemployed. If they are employed, they are frequently working multiple jobs to make ends meet. Transportation problems and child care needs often make simply getting to the instructional setting a major chore. From prior educational experiences, family histories, and cultural backgrounds, many of these learners have become quite skeptical of formal educational programs (Quigley, 1990).

In light of these pressures and demands, successful instructional programs must be designed to maintain and enhance learner motivation (Soifer et al., 1990). Educators of adults have long recognized that relating instructional content to the specific contexts of learners' lives and interests increases motivation to learn (Auerbach, 1989; Fingeret, 1983; Freire, 1970; Rogoff & Lave, 1984; Sticht, 1991). Adults bring to educational programs a wide array of experiences, which they use to help them make sense of what they are trying to learn. For example, some adult learners may not grasp the idea of fractions in mathematics education until they can relate it to some aspect of their family or work experiences. Typically, adults bring a problem focus or orientation to their learning. They want to learn to address a particular problem or issue they are confronting in their lives, and they want to use the information they are learning when dealing with these problems. In other words, adult learning is most effective when it is viewed as *contextual*. By emphasizing learning as contextual, educators also contribute to learners' ability to persist in relatively long commitments to their educational program (Fingeret, 1990).

Within the last several years, several promising approaches that are grounded in the principles of contextual learning have emerged in adult developmental education. Among these approaches are family literacy and Even Start programs (Nickse, 1990), workplace literacy programs (Chase, 1990; Sarmiento & Kay, 1990; Sticht, 1991; Zacharakis-Jutz & Dirkx, 1993), and community-based literacy programs (Fingeret, 1983). In one form or another, these programs rely on an integration of traditional academic content with learners' life contexts (Auerbach, 1992; Freire, 1970; Shor, 1992). That is, in the process of studying and learning about life problems or issues that are important, meaningful, and relevant to them, learners also acquire competence in basic skills areas. Many of these programs show that adults often learn these basic skills more quickly and effectively than in more traditional approaches, which focus on the study of subjects, such as math, reading, or writing.

For example, we once demonstrated the effectiveness of an ITB approach on participation and attendance in an ABE corrections program (Dirkx & Crawford, 1993). The participants in this program had expressed interest in various aspects of the natural world and wanted some of this content included in their instruction. We conducted an experimental instruction program, integrating the teaching of reading skills into these themes.

We selected reading material that focused on the environment and the importance of recycling. We used chapters from science workbooks, articles from newspapers and *National Geographic,* and other texts about the space program to heighten interest in both reading and the natural world. In addition, the instructor used videotapes related to students' interests and constructed games around these themes, using new words and phrases. The learners started an indoor garden to study the various effects of environmental conditions. They initiated a newspaper recycling effort within the classroom and did away with paper and Styrofoam coffee cups, choosing instead to reuse ceramic cups.

Members of the experimental group had over 50 percent more hours and days of attendance than did the control group participants, who received traditional subject matter–focused instruction. In addition, students in the experimental group demonstrated marked gains in desirable reading behaviors.

Thus, there is strong support within the field for ITB instruction for adults in developmental education programs. Scholars and practitioners recognize the potential of this approach for enhancing the meaning of what adults learn and motivating them to persist long enough to complete their goals. The difficulty facing program directors and instructors of adult developmental education, however, is a lack of guidance in the process of successfully integrating academic competencies, such as writing, reading, and math, into the life contexts of their learners. A review of the existing literature suggests a need for practical guides and resource books for teachers who want to use an integrated approach for GED preparation. Relatively little material is available in the form of curriculum guides, handbooks, or actual curricula. Yet, scores of examples of popular education initiatives in literacy and economics education from developing countries indicate the potential for this approach (Freire, 1970; Hope & Timmel, 1984; Kirkness, 1982; Vella, 1994). The goals and objectives used in these approaches are not defined in a traditional manner familiar to the North American practitioner of adult education. However, they provide a successful and useful model for adult learners in developmental education programs.

One recent, promising approach is represented in a project conducted by the ABLE Network in Seattle, Washington (Adult Basic Literacy Educators Network, n.d.). This group has designed a guidebook titled *I*CANS: Integrated Curriculum for Achieving Necessary Skills*. This manual is both similar to and different from our *Guide*. While *I*CANS* also seeks to foster an integrated, thematic approach to curriculum and instruction, the ABLE guidebook is structured around the SCANS (1991) competencies. The individual chapters of *I*CANS* help teachers address these competencies within the context of adult basic and literacy education. It is our view that the present *Guide* complements the approach of the *I*CANS* manual. While *I*CANS* provides a helpful structure for organizing and viewing an integrated and theme-based approach, in this *Guide* we provide more explanation about selecting and identifying themes and share processes to use in integrating traditional academic content more fully with these themes.

Characteristics of an ITB Approach

The approach to adult developmental education described in this *Guide* is grounded in the concept of an integrated approach to curriculum and instruction. Integrating curriculum has received considerable attention in the last several years at all levels of instruction (ASCD, 1991; Brady, 1986, 1989; Brandt, 1991; Brophy & Alleman, 1991; Drake, 1993; Fogarty, 1991, 1992; Gutloff, 1996; Jacobs, 1989, 1991; Kovalik, 1993; Prawat, 1991; Vars, 1991). Much of this effort, however, has been directed at levels of public schooling and encourages *multidisciplinary* or *interdisciplinary* integration (Drake, 1993).

A multidisciplinary approach to integration (Figure 1.1) views the curriculum through the lens of particular disciplines or subject matters. Content from other disciplines may be included to enhance relevance. In the example provided in Figure 1.1, concepts drawn from the various disciplines (see upper part of figure) are taught around the broad theme of the car or the combustion engine. Themes are applied to specific subject areas. Another example would be if teachers used the theme of voting to select relevant reading material for their students. Math teachers may look at how electoral votes and popular votes are computed and compare the two methods.

An interdisciplinary approach (Figure 1.2) shifts the focus away from specific disciplines and stresses disciplinary commonalities. Writing and reading across the disciplines are examples of this form of curriculum integration. Other examples appear in the center of the upper half of Figure 1.2. In both approaches, teachers seek to integrate the content of various subject matters.

The ITB approach is grounded conceptually in a *transdisciplinary* (Figure 1.3) or real-world view of the curriculum. The emphasis here is on increasing meaning and relevance to learners by focusing on their life contexts. As such, the ITB approach differs from traditional approaches to adult developmental education in substantive ways, such as subject-matter or focused approaches. In a focused approach, for example, students would learn to write by composing a business letter. But in an ITB approach, writing a business letter might be only an aspect of a theme unit on "applying for a job"; it would be taught in the context of other basic skills as well. The ITB approach also differs from traditional approaches in the origin of the teacher's activities. In a theme-based approach, teachers begin to develop goals and objectives, curricular materials, teaching strategies, and assessment tools only after they understand the life context and life goals of their learners.

The perspective taken in this *Guide* represents a thematic approach to the education of adults grounded in an experience-based view of learning (Auerbach, 1992; Freire, 1970; Hope & Timmel, 1984; Jarvis, 1992; Shor, 1992; Soifer et al., 1990). An ITB approach represents a way of thinking about and developing instruction in which teachers draw objectives, concepts, and skills from all areas of desired competencies (Ministry of Advanced Education and Job Training, 1987) and integrate them around a general

Figure 1.1.
Multidisciplinary Approach.

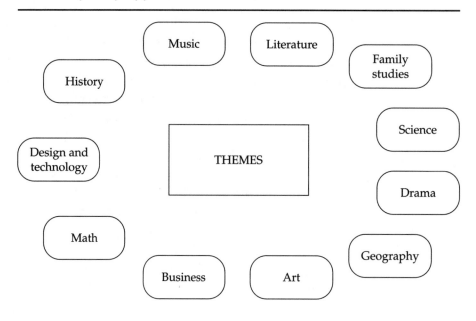

Example

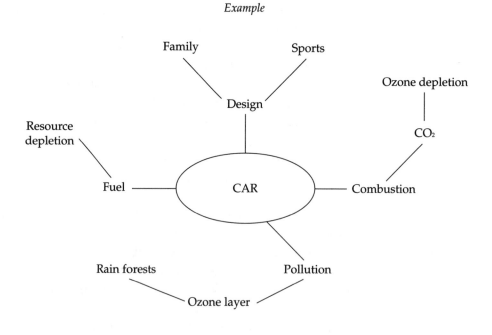

Drake, S. *Planning the Integrated Curriculum: The Call to Adventure*, p. 36. Reprinted by permission of the Association for Supervision and Curriculum Development. Copyright © 1993 by ASCD. All rights reserved.

Figure 1.2.

Interdisciplinary Approach.

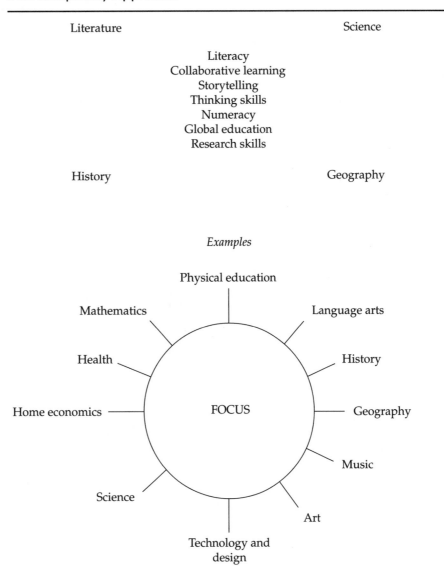

idea or theme that is meaningful to the learner (Gutloff, 1996). The theme must emerge from or speak to the life contexts of the participating learners. Although it represents or connects to concerns of individuals, the instructional theme is an attempt to relocate these concerns within a social context. That is, the theme captures an issue or concern as it is manifested within and shaped by the learners' being together as a community within the instructional setting.

For example, individual learners may be enrolled in a program to increase their chances of getting a job that provides a decent income for their families. "Getting a job" is therefore a concern that

Figure 1.3.
Transdisciplinary Approach.

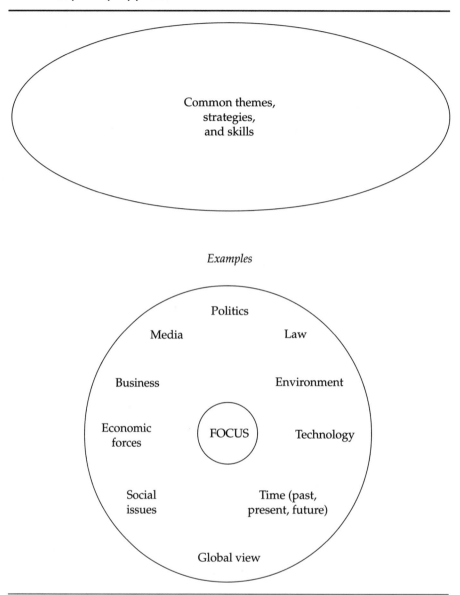

many of the learners share, but the full meaning of this concern only becomes evident as the learners as a group struggle with this issue. As they engage in the topic, they realize that getting a job involves acquiring particular skills and competencies that employers generally value. The theme also provides opportunities for learners to express the ways in which this theme resonates economically and politically within their lives and their communities. In this way, the theme takes them beyond just their individual

Figure 1.4.

Emphasis on a Basic Skill.

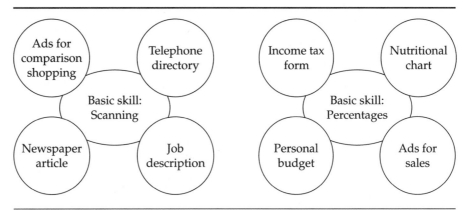

Source: Reprinted with permission from the *I*CANS* Project, Washington State Board for Community & Technical Colleges.

experience of wanting to get a job; "getting a job" becomes a way of analyzing and acting on the socioeconomic and political conditions of their lives.

This approach stresses students' relationship to the content of the materials they are using to learn basic skills, and not just the skills themselves (Fingeret, 1990). According to this research, materials used to teach basic skills, for example, should reflect the personal, work, or community contexts within which those skills will be used. Teachers select from these contexts themes for organizing the curriculum. The theme units recognize what learners already know within these contexts and seek to build on these strengths. Reading, writing, and math skills are all integrated within a single theme grounded in the context of the learners' experiences. The theme directs attention and study to a particular problem, issue, or concern (life skills) within the learners' lives, and the academic skills are used to learn more about this problem or concern. The themes may emerge from the learners, or be selected by the instructor in cooperation with the learners.

In contextual learning, desired competencies or skills in academic subjects, work, or parenting are integrated with specific life contexts. There are, however, several ways to approach this process of contextual learning. Many instructional programs attempting to follow the principles of contextual learning will continue to emphasize the basic skills, such as reading. They will, however, use specific life contexts, such as ads, newspaper articles, and job descriptions to teach these skills. In this perspective on contextual learning, which is often referred to as the "focused approach," objectives, concepts, and activities relate to one area of a particular subject, discipline, or competency (Figure 1.4).

For example, a focused unit might center on strengthening writing skills. The instructor would use the writing of a business letter to teach these skills. The business letter reflects the life context of work-related life skills, and the actual writing of the letter engages the learner in the practice of the academic competencies expected in writing. Similar examples include using the newspaper, the telephone book, or a shop manual to teach particular reading skills, or balancing a checkbook or studying nutritional content listed on food packages to teach certain math skills.

The focused approach to integrating instruction is popular in the education of adults and is widely practiced within developmental programs. When using this approach, however, teachers confront several limitations. While the focused perspective attempts to locate the acquisition of desired competencies within particular life experiences, it tends to reduce these experiences to a series of particular skills. For example, writing a business letter does not just involve writing. Presumably, one is interested in writing such a letter for a particular reason, such as to apply for a job or to complain about service received from a company. These reasons for wanting to write a business letter reflect a social and life context more complex and involved than merely the particular skills emphasized in writing. Reducing this context to both a particular life skill (e.g., the ability to write a business letter) and a particular academic competency (e.g., writing skills) ignores the holistic and multilayered nature of the experiences being represented by the life skill. Although aspects of the learners' life contexts are taken into account in the focused approach, the instruction is not as thoroughly grounded in these contexts as it is with more thematic approaches.

The perspective reflected in Figure 1.5, commonly referred to as a "life skills" approach, attempts to address these limitations and to provide a framework in which basic skills are taught in a more holistic and integrated manner. In this approach, life skills are not used as a means of illustrating the use of basic skills but rather as the ends of instruction themselves. Basic skills become a means through which these ends are achieved but are not taught independently or one at a time, as in the case of the focused approach.

The life skills perspective represented in Figure 1.5 is similar to the process advocated in this *Guide*. In this approach, a particular skill that learners need within the contexts of their lives becomes the focus of instruction, and basic skills are used to help develop and enhance that life skill. For example, selecting a balanced diet may be a skill learners are seeking to develop. The instructor recognizes, however, the multilayered nature of this learning activity. Learning to balance one's diet involves particular

Figure 1.5.

Emphasis on a Life Skill Competency.

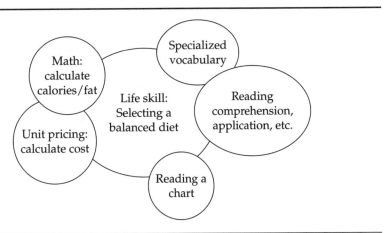

Source: Reprinted with permission from the *I*CANS* Project, Washington State Board for Community & Technical Colleges.

kinds of math, reading, and language skills, and these must be taught in an integrated manner as the learner seeks to develop competency in maintaining a balanced diet. The end goal is selecting a balanced diet, but in the process the learner will acquire a number of basic skills as well.

In our opinion, however, the life skills approach still does not fully conceptualize instruction within the context of learners' lives. Frequently, these "life skills" have been identified prior to instruction and deemed important by others external to the learning experience (e.g., in the practice of many workplace literacy programs). That is, despite their label, life skills become *decontextualized* from the learners' lives and are regarded as skills that learners must acquire in order to succeed in life. In this sense, the skills are viewed as separate from learners' lives—the very lives they are meant to improve.

While they are closer conceptually to the contexts of particular learners than in the focused approach, life skills as they are represented in Figure 1.5 do not fully address the sociocultural, economic, and political contexts in which learners find themselves. The life skills approach tends to emphasize acquisition of important skills such as problem solving, critical thinking, and learning-to-learn, as well as basic competencies. But it tends to ignore other important process skills connected with the social context of learning and living, such as working as part of group or team, interpersonal communication skills, creativity, and the ability to negotiate among conflicting perspectives or demands.

The ITB approach we are advocating in this *Guide* is illustrated in Figure 1.6. In this approach, *academic competencies* are taught in an integrated manner with life skills and process skills within contexts relevant and meaningful to learners' life experiences (Auerbach, 1992; Freire, 1970; Kovalik, 1993; Ministry of Advanced Education and Job Training, 1987). By academic competencies, we are referring to intellectual knowledge and skills defined within a particular domain or discipline. They are largely defined by particular subject matters or content areas. For example, in adult secondary education or GED preparation programs, academic skills refer to competencies that students need in order to pass the GED tests in reading (literature and the arts), writing, math, science, and social studies. The term *basic skills* refers to those academic competencies that lower-level ABE instruction addresses. Although calling certain skills "academic" is conceptual and somewhat arbitrary, we feel the distinction is useful when thinking about the various levels or dimensions of learning that are possible in adult education. The distinction between academic skills and other skills, such as life and process skills, provides some guidance in developing and planning instruction. There are no definitive grade-level equivalencies that distinguish these two sets of skills. However, for the purposes of this project, the term *basic skills* generally refers to those academic competencies reflected in grade-level equivalencies less than six. Grade-level equivalencies between seven and eleven in math and reading, as determined by the TABE, are considered the domain of GED and pre-GED skills preparation. (See Resource A at the end of this book for a listing of academic and life-skills competencies, workplace competencies, and the interrelationship between these categories of skills.)

Process skills refer to competencies that learners use when engaging in the learning process or other experiences within their life contexts. Recent literature, as well as federal policy, has emphasized the importance of problem-solving, critical thinking and learning-to-learn skills in developmental education programs for adults. Rather than teach these important skills as separate and decontextualized from academic skills and life experiences, the ITB approach fully integrates such skills with these other areas. In addition, the ITB approach includes other important process skills, such as interpersonal communication, teamwork, brainstorming, and creativity. Academic and process skills are then taught within particular contexts that serve to shape the overall tenor and tone of the learning experience. Through this integrated approach, learners increase their academic skills and enhance important process skills, while addressing issues in their lives that are important and meaningful to them. At the core of the experience are the learners and the themes that represent salient aspects of their collective life experiences.

We refer to the graphic representation in Figure 1.6 as the

Figure 1.6.
The Spinning Top.

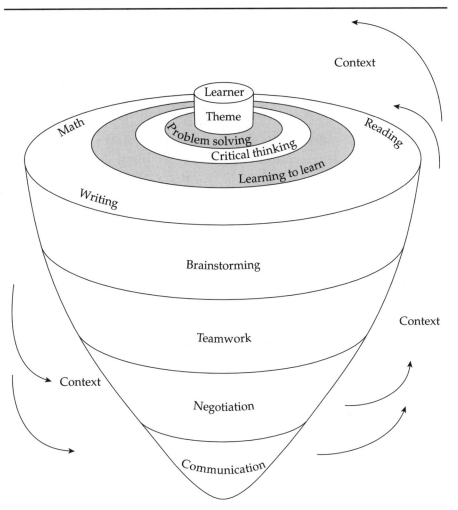

"spinning top" model of ITB instruction for adults. This model is a way of thinking about what you are teaching. The central notion of this model is that it integrates academic skills, life skills, and the processes of problem solving, learning-to-learn, and critical thinking into the learning setting, using the learners themselves as a point of departure. Imagine a brightly colored spinning top. At the core is the learner. She begins to spin through the educational process. At the beginning of the first turn, she states her goals and wishes for learning. She speaks of her life. She shares her history. From this first spin comes the theme that you will develop together. With each spin you learn more about her skills and capacities. Together, you develop learning objectives. She acquires new skills as she spins through experiences and activities that have been designed to help her achieve her goals. You, the teacher, facilitate the process by guiding her through new terrain. Imagine yourself to be the hand that reaches out to spin the top, mixing in the skills and processes that need to be learned.

For example, your adult learners may identify "getting a job" as a primary concern (life skill). You would identify academic competencies or basic skills relevant to or included in the theme area. Then, you would plan and select curriculum and instruction to foster mastery of these basic or academic skills, as well as the process skills, within the broader context of the themes selected. In this sense, you integrate the academic skills into the themes that compose the curriculum. All of this work, however, takes place with the learner at the center of the instructional process, taking into account the social, political, cultural, and economic contexts in which that life is immersed.

As we indicated earlier, developmental education programs for adults have traditionally stressed a subject-matter approach within their instruction. That is, they emphasize the mastery of academic content within specific, clearly delineated subject matter or content areas. Increasingly, however, educators have begun to draw on the contexts of learners' experiences to teach basic skills, particularly in such programs as basic workplace skills, family literacy, and ESL. In adult high school or GED preparation programs, though, there remains a stronger tendency to structure teaching around the five specific subjects that make up the GED tests. Because many students and practitioners view the curriculum as "test-driven," instructors may find it difficult to design learning experiences not considered directly "relevant" to the knowledge needed to pass the test. The present *Guide* is intended to offer assistance to programs that have been traditionally viewed as subject-centered. In particular, the Resources at the end of the book show how practitioners may bridge the gap between the competencies expressed through the GED test and other measures of life skills, such as those defined by the Secretary's Commission on Achieving Necessary Skills (SCANS) and the Comprehensive Adult Student Assessment System (CASS).

Tips for Using the *Guide*

Like adult learners, educators of adults vary in their training, experience level, skill with various approaches, and interests. For some, the *Guide* will be "old hat," and will stimulate thinking on issues involved in integrating thematic instruction, life skills, and academic competencies. For others, it will take some time to become familiar with all that teaching from an ITB perspective involves.

Thinking about how to learn an ITB approach reminds one of us of her grandmother's approach to teaching young ones how to cook. Grandmother used a fistful of this and a pinch of that. Measurements were in terms of "just enough," or "more or less." In teaching others how to cook, she would advise, "just enough water, two tablespoons of flour, more or less." The dishes that resulted never turned out quite the same as hers, but they were just as successful. Those who have participated in this kind of training readily recognize that the written-down recipes were deliciously imprecise. While some may find this lack of precision frustrating, others find room for experimentation and innovation.

The metaphor of cooking seems helpful in this case. This *Guide* is not intended to be a cookbook that can or should be followed religiously. Rather, it is meant to be used as needed, adjusted to different requirements and styles, reacted to, marked up, revised, and reconstructed. Our hope is that this book provides a stimulus for encompassing an ITB approach in the education of adults.

Some general guidelines may be helpful in getting you into the *Guide*. The first three chapters of the book are intended to provide a conceptual or theoretical foundation for the ideas presented in subsequent chapters. With Chapter Four, we begin to focus more specifically on the tasks, methods, and strategies associated with this approach to instruction. Chapters Five through Seven continue this theme, focusing specifically on different aspects of the instructional process and its assessment. We conclude our discussion of ITB instruction in Chapter Eight by naming and discussing the challenges and opportunities that this approach presents. The Resources at the end of the book are for you to consult as you see fit.

If you have little formal training in working with adults, you may want to read the discussion carefully about the meaning of contextual learning in adulthood (Chapter Two), how learning styles influence what, how, and why we learn (Chapter Two), and what it means to provide instruction from this perspective (Chapter Three). For those of you who have been working with adult learners for some time, you may just want to review these theoretical chapters, perhaps focusing specifically on the rationale for this approach. For those of you who have found yourselves intuitively practicing this approach or something like it, reading Chapters One, Two, and Three may provide a deeper understanding of the philosophical assumptions that have guided your intuitive practice. Others who are familiar with the meaning of contextual learning and thematic instruction may wish to proceed straight to the chapters on instructional strategies and assessment (Four through Seven). Those wishing to pursue this approach to instruction in more depth can use the References to augment this study.

Our strong recommendation is not to plan on changing your instructional approach overnight. Together with other program staff and even some interested adult learners, you need to develop an overall, flexible plan for implementing this approach. This plan should reflect the economic, political, and social realities of your particular program. You need to ask about the levels of support available within the program for this kind of change. Programmatic and peer support are important in effectively implementing ITB instruction. We encourage you, if at all possible, to work with others in your program who may be interested in the philosophy and the methods represented by ITB instruction. Planning should involve careful reflection on how you learn about your students, including who they are, what they have told you about their past experiences, and what their hopes and fears are. We recommend that you practice ways to probe multiple facets of a theme and monitor your comfort levels and emotional responses to these different aspects. Finally, we encourage you to participate in workshops and other professional development opportunities that focus on integrating curriculum or instruction for adults.

A worksheet covering the various ideas discussed in this chapter is provided in Exhibit 1.1 to help you get started.

Exhibit 1.1.
Getting Started.

1. Think of your own goals and objectives for implementing ITB instruction. Jot them down.

   _____

   _____

   _____

2. Reflect on what you are trying to teach. How do these ideas mesh with your goals for ITB instruction?

   _____

   _____

   _____

3. What are some of the ways in which your learners talk about or state their own educational goals? What are they hoping to accomplish through this study?

   _____

   _____

   _____

4. In what ways do these educational goals represent your learners' life contexts or life experiences? What do these goals say about the ways in which your learners make sense of their learning?

   _____

   _____

   _____

5. What opportunities for teaching academic competencies, life skills, and process skills do these stated goals and objectives represent?

   _____

   _____

   _____

6. How might you address your thoughts about teaching and about your learners' educational goals in an ITB approach to instruction?

   _____

   _____

   _____

CHAPTER 2

Understanding Contextual Learning in Educating Adults

Recently, one of us led a workshop on the adult learner. For this session, there were assigned readings that focused on adult development and its influence on learning. During the break, a student approached the workshop leader, pointing out a short summary in the readings on transitions in adulthood. She remarked, "This is amazing. This is me. I can see myself in each of these steps they describe here. I have never quite understood the feelings I've had with these changes I have made recently, but this really helps me make sense of all that I have been through." In an excited and joyful manner, she spent several minutes elaborating on how this brief description had given her a deeper understanding of a transition from which she was just emerging. As she talked, she gave the impression that a light had been shone over a confusing part of her life.

This anecdote illustrates how powerful learning can be when it is grounded in and connected to the context and meaning of adults' lives, an idea referred to as *contextual learning*. ITB instruction is based on contextual learning. Simply put, contextual learning refers to learning that students find meaningful, relevant, and significant to their situations and life experiences (Auerbach, 1989; Rogoff & Lave, 1984; Shor, 1992). The content of learning reflects the learners' contexts and life situations. Contextual learning emphasizes the construction of personal meaning within the act of learning.

The purpose of this chapter is to provide an overview of contextual learning and how it relates to ITB instruction in developmental education for adults. We will discuss characteristics of adult learning, the concept of active learning, and how learning styles are manifest among learners. We first provide a summary of key points for each of these sections, and then elaborate these points further in a traditional narrative form.

Importance of Experience and Meaning in Adult Learning _____

- Adults often read to learn about some aspect of their real world. They "read to learn," rather than "learn to read." (For example, they read to learn about how to care for their newborn infant, what the country of their ancestors is like, and what careers are available in the fields that match their interests.)

- Adults learn within their concrete life experiences. These experiences are both a resource and a medium for their learning.

- An adult's sense of self will influence what he or she learns and how he or she learns it.

In *Effective Teaching and Mentoring* (1986), Larry Daloz suggests that adults seek out education in part to help them make sense of "lives whose fabric of meaning has grown frayed" (p. 1). The material and strategies presented in this *Guide* are based on the idea that participating in educational programs is a way in which adults make sense of their life experiences. It is often helpful to consider the nature of adults as learners and how adults learn in the contexts of their lives. Over the last several years, we have spoken with many individuals about their experiences as adults returning to continue education. One man, whom we will call Jake, participated in a pilot educational project on integrated, thematic instruction. Jake provides a perspective on learning that closely reflects the assumptions of the ITB approach to learning.

Sitting in the bright classroom of the prison school, Jake did not seem like the "typical" inmate doing time in a maximum security facility. A slender African American in his early twenties with a studious but gentle demeanor, Jake was one of over twenty students in the school's adult basic education (ABE) program. He agreed to talk with us about his experiences in the instructional project. In an uncertain, halting manner, he first spoke of his goals for being in the program:

The knowledge, with learning, to better myself as a person, to improve my skills on reading, math, all the things one needs to accomplish the GED and to go further in college.

Like so many new adult readers, Jake struggled between wanting to learn to read and feeling too ashamed to admit to anyone that he couldn't read. Traditional instructional methods have been based on the assumption that one first must "learn to read and then read to learn" (Fingeret, 1990, p. 27). These traditional methods stress the importance of developing literacy skills as a prerequisite to acquiring other information and skills. Specific circumstances, experiences, and the sociocultural contexts of the learners' lives are considered secondary to acquiring reading skills, if they are considered at all.

With the help of a caring instructor, however, Jake realized that "it's not a shame to admit it," and found that learning to read was really a way of learning-to-learn: "Once you get beyond that point, then you learn how to start to learn." Now he looks to the ABE program as a way of helping him learn new things about his world:

> Once you start learning and begin to learn, then the doors begin to open and it improves you as a person because when you can't read, you stay shelter[ed]. You don't look beyond that point. . . . Reading allows you to know what's going on in the world way beyond where you are at and to allow you to see the difference and read about it, not just the normal view that you would normally have if you couldn't read.

Learning as Active and Context-Based

- Students are active in the learning process. They are involved in doing things that are relevant and meaningful to them, and they learn through doing.
- Learning is viewed as a process of making sense or meaning of real-life contexts and experiences that learners bring to the educational setting.
- In the ITB approach, students actively participate in deciding what they should learn and how they should learn it.
- When engaged in active learning, students use skills such as reading, writing, and computing to identify and solve problems within their own life contexts.
- In the ITB approach, learners construct their own knowledge, rather than being recipients of others' knowledge.

- In active learning, the teacher is a "guide on the side" rather than a "sage on the stage."

Jake captures what many adult literacy educators claim as the overall aim of their instruction—to foster reading as a way of learning about and opening up whole new worlds for adult learners. He recognizes the interrelationship between learning to read and understanding his own life contexts. Jake reads to learn about these contexts and his experiences within them.

The learner's life contexts and experiences are central to grounding learning in an ITB curriculum. In this approach, academic content, such as reading, writing, and math skills, is fully integrated within selected themes, which represent important aspects of the learner's experiences. Thus, the academic skills are used within contexts that are real, relevant, and meaningful to the learner.

Along with the other learners in the reading program, Jake expressed an interest in knowing about the natural world. As he learned to read, Jake also gained knowledge about the effects of global warming on tropical rain forests and other areas of the earth. He read about recycling and, together with his fellow students, implemented a process for recycling newspapers within the classroom. After reading about the effects of acid rain, the students conducted an experiment with garden plants to demonstrate what acidic conditions can do to normal plant life. No one in this group really articulated the particular reasons that they were so fascinated with studying the natural world. It is likely, however, that such an interest provided a means of transcending the conditions of their present context—confinement and separation from the outer world. Reading was a way to connect with a broader world immediately outside the prison walls, as well as far beyond in the incomprehensible spaces of the Milky Way.

In describing his goals for learning, Jake illustrates the importance of *meaning* in the learning process. When reading to learn, we try to make sense of our experiences in the world. These experiences provide a lens through which we filter new information. The lens gives us a way to understand these learning experiences. In his book *Fantasy and Feeling in Education* (1968), child psychologist Richard Jones underscores how important it is that we understand the lenses that our learners use to make meaning of their life contexts.

Jones recounts the story of an eight-year-old boy named Billy who had been referred to him by a local school district. Billy had something of a reputation among the teachers for not paying attention in class and, at times, even being somewhat disruptive. Many regarded him as "behaviorally disordered." One day, the teacher was telling the class about the concept of infinity and asked the children if any of them knew what infinity meant. After some trepidation, Billy raised his hand and the teacher called on him. He hesitated and initially stuttered as he began to reply. "Uh, I think it's like a box of Cream of Wheat." Assuming that Billy was up to his usual antics, the teacher replied, "Billy, don't be silly!"

In a later session with Billy, Jones had been visiting with the young "troublemaker" about this incident for some time when it occurred to him to ask Billy why he thought infinity was like a box of Cream of Wheat. "Billy," Jones asked tentatively, "*how* is infinity like box of Cream of Wheat?" "Well," Billy proceeded, "think of a box of Cream of Wheat. It shows a man holding a box of Cream of Wheat. Right? And that box shows the same man holding the same box. Right? And that box. . . .You can't see them all, like you can't see infinity. You just know they're all there, going on forever and ever" (Jones, 1968, pp. 72, 75–76).

How many times have *we* felt the need to relate abstract ideas or concepts to something with which we are familiar, something that we know about or with which we can identify? Billy was attempting to take a complex idea and think about it in ways that were meaningful for him. For Billy, learning about infinity required a context or a lens through which he could *experience* infinity. Recalling the many times that he stared at a box of Cream of Wheat over breakfast provided that lens. Although this story is drawn from the experiences of a young boy in elementary school, it represents a powerful lesson about how our learners struggle with making sense of what we try to teach them. One of the most powerful ways to make learning meaningful is to ground the teaching-learning process in the life experiences of the adult learners.

Larry is a middle-aged, white man who works as a laborer. At the time we met him, he was also a student in an adult basic education class that met two evenings each week in the upper floor of a community center. His attendance had been somewhat erratic because of the demands from his job and family. The group had just recently formed and had met only several times, but before this evening, Larry had missed two sessions.

On this particular night, Larry worked on learning fractions. He sat alone in the corner of the room, clearly having difficulties with this area of study. When he raised his hand to request assistance, he seemed frustrated and ready to throw in the towel. The volunteer asked him what he was working on and he replied "mixed fractions" in a voice filled with frustration and distaste for this learning task. But then he proceeded to say, "This happens to me all the time. I work on them for a while, think I got it, but then when I come back next time, it's like I don't remember any of it."

Selecting one of the problems, the volunteer asked a few questions about which fraction was smaller or larger, but Larry seemed unable to answer the questions. "Fractions," he said in desperation, "make no sense."

Then the volunteer asked Larry if he had a socket set at home. "Sure," he said, "I use them all the time." The volunteer suggested, "Think of these fractions as the different kinds of sockets in your tool chest. You have a $\frac{3}{8}$" socket and you have a $\frac{1}{2}$" socket. Which of these is larger?" Almost without thinking about it, Larry responded, "The $\frac{1}{2}$" socket is larger." The volunteer affirmed his response and then used several more examples like this, drawing from Larry's work with tools. It soon became apparent that Larry was able to recognize which of the mixed fractions were larger or smaller. As he worked in this vein, Larry relaxed and grew more confident with his work on fractions. He told the volunteer, "I think I get it now," and proceeded to work the problems.

The volunteer used Larry's life context in teaching examples, providing Larry with assurance that he already had experience with fractions. These experiences provided a meaningful and visual prompt from which Larry could draw as he continued to learn about mixed fractions. Figure 2.1 provides a graphic illustration of how learning activities influence how much people acquire. When learners are involved only in verbal or visual receiving, they remember less than 50 percent of what they see and hear. When they are involved in hearing, saying, seeing, and doing, learners retain much higher levels of information.

In the ITB curriculum, practitioners facilitate *active learning*. This term refers to what students are doing within the instructional process. Students who are active in the learning process are writing, discussing, or engaging in problem solving, thereby using higher-order thinking skills (Bonwell & Eison, 1991). When engaged in active learning, students are doing things and thinking about what they are doing. Several studies demonstrate that students prefer active learning to more traditional, passive forms of learning. In addition, studies have shown that using active learning strategies, including mastery of content and development of thinking and writing skills, affects student achievement positively.

When learning is active, students can use relevant life experiences as a source of learning and as a way of helping each other. That is, they *construct* meaning from their life experiences in relation to the topics they are studying. Traditionally, practitioners have relied on a received form of meaning, in which the meaning of the subject at hand is derived from experts, texts, or other sources of authority. In ITB instruction, however, learning is

Figure 2.1.
Cone of Experience.

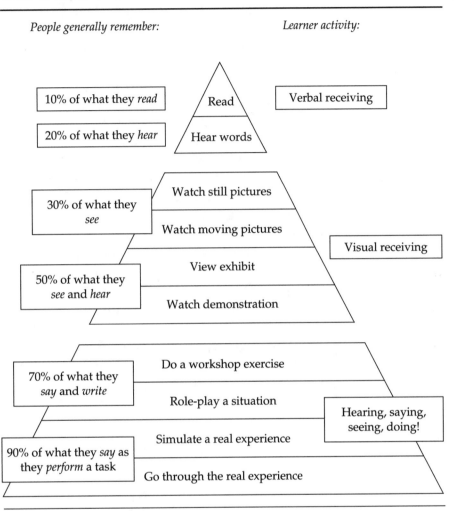

People generally remember: *Learner activity:*

10% of what they *read*   Read   Verbal receiving

20% of what they *hear*   Hear words

30% of what they *see*   Watch still pictures

                               Watch moving pictures   Visual receiving

50% of what they *see* and *hear*   View exhibit

                               Watch demonstration

70% of what they *say* and *write*   Do a workshop exercise

                               Role-play a situation   Hearing, saying, seeing, doing!

90% of what they *say* as they *perform* a task   Simulate a real experience

                               Go through the real experience

Source: Adapted from E. Dale, *Audiovisual Methods in Teaching* (New York: Dryden Press, 1954, p. 43).

viewed as a process in which learners use their own life contexts and experiences to construct meanings from what they are studying. The story of Billy and the box of Cream of Wheat illustrates this idea.

If learning is to be active and meaning is to be constructed within the learning experience, the educational process must be *learner-centered.* What the student will learn and how the student will learn it must arise, at least in part, from the learner's experiences, life contexts, needs, and interests. The instructor is less the "sage on the stage" than a "guide on the side." Many developmental education programs for adults try hard to take the learners' particular needs, interests, preferences, and abilities into account when planning their courses of study. That is, they individualize the curriculum and adapt their instructional approaches to individual differences among learners. The ITB approach to curriculum, however, actively involves the learners in a *participatory* way in selecting what is to be learned and how. This characteristic is clearly illustrated in the process of identifying and selecting themes (see Chapter Four) around which instruction is to be organized.

The importance of learner participation and involvement in the design and implementation of learning experiences is reflected in numerous works on adult learning and popular education. These ideas are powerfully illustrated in a wonderful, small book by Jane Vella (1994), *Learning to Listen, Learning to Teach.* In a very readable style, Vella discusses twelve basic principles of adult learning. Using her forty–plus years of experience teaching adults in the United States, Africa, Asia, Latin America, and the Middle East, Vella illustrates with specific examples how learner involvement and participation are fundamental to each of these twelve principles. From designing and conducting an assessment of training needs in Ethiopia, to fostering action and reflection in a community development program in the Maldives in the Indian Ocean, to engaging hospice staff in learning in North Carolina, her case studies reveal the power of the learners' voices in the process of learning. Vella shows how, when students authentically participate in learning, it enriches the experience for all involved.

Learning Styles Among Adult Learners

- Learning styles reflect overall patterns, involving behaviors and attitudes, that provide direction for teaching and learning.

- Each learner is born with certain tendencies that are also shaped by culture, personal experiences, maturation, and development.

- Differences in style may be manifest in cognitive, affective, and physiological factors that influence the learning process.

- Understanding learning styles better can help teachers reduce frustration for themselves and their students.

- Taking learning styles into account can help motivate learners, improve their self-concepts, and increase achievement.

- Teachers who incorporate learning styles can plan more appropriate learning experiences for their students.

- An emphasis on learning styles can also lead to diverse ways of learning and flexibility among learners.
- Communication is enhanced when learning styles are incorporated into the learning setting.

It is clear from our discussion thus far that learners' experiences are central to the instructional process in an ITB approach. This focus also includes understanding students' particular preferences for ways of learning, or what many refer to as "learning styles." The teachers who participated in our project affirmed the importance of considering individual learning styles as a central part of an ITB approach.

It is beyond the scope of this *Guide* to provide anything more than an overview of the issue of learning styles. Many good resources are available that explain in more detail various learning styles and how teachers might adapt instruction to address differences in style among their learners. The References at the end of this book list a few resources that focus more specifically on the nature of learning styles and how teachers can accommodate these differences within their instruction (Gardner, 1983; Presseisen, Sternberg, Fischer, Knight, & Feuerstein, 1990; Reiff, 1992). In this section, we will simply define what we mean by learning styles, why they are important in adult learning, and how they may be manifest in an adult learning situation.

Learning styles are defined and classified in many different ways (Reiff, 1992). In general, they refer to

> overall patterns that provide direction to learning and teaching. Learning styles can also be described as a set of factors, behaviors, and attitudes that facilitate learning for an individual in a given situation . . . the style may be unique to the task, or it may duplicate a previous experience (p. 7).

Learning styles will influence how adults learn, the kinds of instruction that teachers give them, and the ways in which teachers and learners interact. While it is thought that each person is born with certain styles, these tendencies are influenced by the cultures in which we live, the personal experiences we have in education, and processes of maturation and development. Style is considered a "contextual" variable, because it reflects what the learner brings to the particular learning experience.

Styles may differ along cognitive, affective, and physiological dimensions (Merriam & Caffarella, 1991; Reiff, 1992). *Cognitive style* refers to the ways in which one perceives, remembers, thinks, and solves problems—that is, the focus is on *how* one learns, rather than *what* one learns. There are several ways to understand and measure cognitive style, and each method expresses a slightly different aspect of how learners approach a particular learning task cognitively. For example, one learner may be highly global in the way she approaches a problem, while another may be very analytic. Some learners are impulsive and want to act right away, while others are more reflective and want to take their time and think about a problem before acting.

Learners may also differ in their orientation to the field in which the learning task is embedded. To learn effectively, some learners need structure, depend on others for support and feedback, and prefer social learning settings. Learners with these preferences are sometimes bothered by crowded or busy worksheets. Others, however, seem less attached to these field elements, focusing on the task independent of these external factors. They often prefer to work alone and to chart their own course within the learning experience. Cognitive style may also be expressed in learners' preferences for visual, auditory, tactile, or kinesthetic modes. While some learners may prefer the written word, others want to hear words spoken or to act out the lesson in some manner.

The sharp dichotomies that have been used here to illustrate different cognitive approaches to a learning task are seldom seen in the "real world." Often, learners express aspects of both dimensions of a given continuum, but will demonstrate a preference or tendency toward one or the other of the contrasting ways of learning.

Affective style involves personality and emotional characteristics, including such things as persistence, locus of control, responsibility, motivation, and interaction with peers. Examples of affective styles include conceptual levels and the psychological types identified through the Myers-Briggs Type Indicator (MBTI) (Cranton, 1994).

Learners may differ in their conceptual levels and will respond differently to conflict and authority within the learning setting. For example, adults at conceptual level one may be less flexible in their orientation to the structure of their learning environment and may be more evaluative of this environment. They may not readily accept dramatic changes or departures in what they have come to believe about learning or the ways in which teaching and learning should be organized. Their responses to others within the environment seem fixed and they may experience some difficulties in their relations with the instructor or other learners. Learners with conceptual levels of three or four may be more open to alternatives and may seem to defer judgment or evaluation of their environment and the people within it. As a result, they use or are able to develop good interpersonal skills. These differences in how individuals impose structure on their learning environment often become readily apparent in group work and in tasks that are ambiguous or uncertain. While some learners seem to thrive in these environments and find them intellectually and emotionally stimulating, others quickly become frustrated and annoyed with the instructor and with other group members who seem to support this kind of learning environment.

Affective preferences for learning are expressed through personality differences as well, such as the psychological types identified through the MBTI. Psychological type theory is derived from the work of Carl Jung and has been used by educators of adults (e.g., Cranton, 1994, 1996) to understand better how personality characteristics influence and shape students' behavior within learning environments. Type theory identifies four ways in which people approach and perceive situations in their lives and make decisions about these situations. People can be classified as: sensing, intuitive, thinking, or feeling.

Sensing types see the world in concrete and real terms. They like detail and use their senses to gather information and learn about their world. People of this type are interested in facts rather than theory, specific observations rather than hunches or guesses. Intuitive types like to imagine, invent, and solve problems. They are attracted to new events or new ways of doing things, are less patient with routine or traditional patterns of experience, and tend to be global in their orientation to learning tasks. Within a reading class, for example, the contrast between these two types might show up as differences in what kinds of reading material learners prefer, such as nonfiction versus fiction.

Preferences in decision making are also manifested through different types. A thinking type will be more objective when making decisions. Learners of this type will emphasis fairness and logical procedures and insist that the decision making not become a personal issue. Often, they may seem more interested in ideas than in people.

On the other hand, learners of the feeling type will often stress the subjective and emotional components of a decision-making situation and will base their decisions more on insight and emotions than on reason and logic. Frequently, it is hard for feeling types to disagree with others, and they sometimes find themselves siding simultaneously with two people who are violently disagreeing with each other. For example, if the learning group is trying to make a decision about a specific learning task, and there are polarized positions manifest within the group, the feeling type may find himself torn between these subgroups. Within the discussion, this person will continuously remind the group of the personal and subjective dimensions of the problem they are addressing.

Physiological style is biologically based and relates to things like differences between genders and preferences for environmental characteristics, such as light and temperature. Physiological style is often reflected, for example, in preferences for morning, afternoon, or evening activities, needs for breaks, and desire for background music. Some younger adult learners may be quite used to having background music while they study and the emphasis on quiet environments in some adult learning settings may be more of a distraction than noise. For this reason, it is often a good idea within developmental education programs for adults to have some options available, such as a room in which individuals who desire a quiet environment are able to work, and different lighting or temperature conditions, if possible.

Each of these different ways of expressing preferences for learning in adulthood is also influenced by educational achievement, age, race, and gender, but it is more difficult to generalize about the influence of these variables on learning styles (Reiff, 1992). For example, research clearly indicates that culture will influence various aspects of an adult's approach to learning, but the differences between people may be as great as, or greater than, the differences across cultural groups. Gender is another variable that may influence how individuals approach a learning task, but there are varying opinions among researchers about the extent of this influence.

Tips for Designing Instruction

To summarize this chapter, we have listed several suggestions for designing and implementing instruction for adults. We derived some of the ideas presented below from the *I*CANS* report (Adult Basic Literacy Educators Network, n.d.), while others reflect our own experience and understanding of how to facilitate adult learning:

- Let students know what they are to learn and why they are learning it so that they can understand both the immediate and long-term usefulness of the training or education to their lives

- When teaching new material, build on knowledge that the student had before entering the program.

- Sequence new lessons so that they incorporate material from previous lessons.

- Integrate instruction in reading, writing, arithmetic, and problem solving into academic or technical training programs to enhance transfer of knowledge. Avoid decontextualized basic skills "remedial" programs.

- Choose objectives after analyzing the knowledge and skills that the learner needs in situations for which he or she is preparing.

- As much as possible, work with contexts, tasks, materials, and procedures taken from the setting in which the learner will be functioning.

- Enrich and modify your curricular and instructional materials to accommodate a wide diversity of preferences for learning.

- Avoid judging learners because of their particular preferences or approaches to learning. Remember that there are multiple ways to approach a given learning task.

CHAPTER 3

Defining the Teacher's Role in Thematic Instruction

In this chapter, we will discuss several general principles of instruction reflected in the ITB approach. Our purpose here is to provide a conceptual understanding for designing and implementing instruction that uses this approach. In Chapter Four, we discuss the specific issues related to identifying, selecting, and planning theme units, while Chapter Six describes specific instructional strategies that can be used with the ITB approach. The topics to be covered in this chapter include effective teacher-learner relationships, effective facilitation, context-based instruction, collaborative learning, and adapting instruction to styles of learning.

Characteristics of Effective Teacher-Learner Relationships _____

- Good teaching reflects care for learners.
- Caring teachers are concerned with developing the whole person, rather than just helping learners acquire knowledge and skills.
- Effective teachers become mentors to their adult learners.
- Mentors support, challenge, and provide vision to their learners.

The relationship instructors establish with their students is one of the most important dimensions of developmental education for adults (Daloz, 1986; Vella, 1994). Many experienced instructors in this field express this relationship in terms of caring for their students and they indicate that caring instructors are the most significant characteristic of a quality program (Dirkx, 1995). One of the instructors who shared her time and views with us about ITB instruction commented that her relationships with students were perhaps the most important aspect of her instructional approach.

This view of education as caring is reflected in the literature on effective teaching in adult education. For example, Daloz (1986) argues that education should be about the *development* of the whole person, not merely the acquisition of knowledge or skills. From a developmental perspective, "The central element of good teaching becomes the provision of *care* rather than the use of teaching skills or transmission of knowledge" (p. xvii). Teaching is "a special kind of relationship, a caring stance in the moving context of our students' lives" (p. 14). All instructors who work with adults over time face the deeper question, "What is my place in the growth of those I care for?" (p. 15).

Daloz suggests that we think of teaching as occurring within a caring relationship that attends to the movement of our learners' lives. Attending to this movement takes us as instructors beyond just helping them acquire knowledge to pass the GED or develop life skills. To frame this relationship with a powerful metaphor, instructors are guides or mentors in the learner's journey. The power of the mentoring relationship is reflected in such films as the *Star Wars* trilogy, *Stand and Deliver*, *Dead Poets Society*, and *Fried Green Tomatoes*. For example, in *The Empire Strikes Back*, Yoda is a small gnomelike creature who provides Luke Skywalker, the hero, with the knowledge he will need to save the galaxy from the destructive powers of Evil. In his role as Luke's mentor, Yoda confirms Luke's importance in this battle, challenges Luke's ability, and reminds him of his destiny.

Daloz (1986) suggests that, as mentors to our students, we play a similar role. He identifies three functions of effective mentors: (1) to support, (2) to challenge, and (3) to provide vision. When we act as mentors, learners feel supported, cared about, and cared for. Our relationship reflects our willingness to understand them. Within this relationship, they establish a basic sense of trust. We confirm their self-worth and accept them where they are. We actively listen to their stories, provide needed structure in their learning environment, express positive expectations, advocate for them, and share ourselves. One student we talked with described the support his teacher provided:

She has worked with me. On a personal level, she has been there, to be my overseer on things that I neglected. She has saved me from a lot of misery. She has stayed with me and worked with me.

As their relationships develop, mentors challenge their learners. Significant learning and change will occur only when students experience novelty. Teachers make this happen by introducing contradictory ideas, questioning learner assumptions, and sometimes even refusing to answer certain questions. Through the process of challenge, teachers open a space between the learner and his or her environment. They create a tension within the student that calls for closure. Challenge always takes place within a context of support.

To mentor their students effectively, teachers need to aim for the right blend of support and challenge for each learner (Daloz, 1986). In one of the group sessions we observed, Sue Ellen, a student in the program, reported a problem in her living situation. She had apparently lost her keys. She suspected that one of her neighbors, with whom she thought she had a good relationship, had found the keys but was not returning them. Rather than simply advising Sue Ellen on what to do, the teacher used this opportunity to help Sue Ellen and the learning group approach this situation from a problem-solving perspective. Together, they explored the issue more fully, discussed ways in which Sue Ellen could approach this problem, and helped her reach a decision about specific actions to take. In this episode, the teacher provided the necessary support for Sue Ellen and the group, but also challenged her to question behaviors and habits that led to such occurrences and to explore new ways of acting.

As mentors, teachers provide vision for their learners. They encourage them to see new possibilities, directions, purposes, and meanings. They help learners look ahead, dream, and sketch their own maps. They aid students in naming the changes they are experiencing and assist them in playing out the conversation that they have between the old self and the new self. In Chapter Two, Jake spoke of how his teacher, by helping him learn to read, provided him with vision:

> Reading allows you to know what's going on in the world way beyond where you are at and to allow you to see the difference and read about it, not just the normal view that you would normally have if you couldn't read.

Mentoring is a powerful means of viewing the teacher-learner relationship. It takes us as educators beyond roles traditionally assumed for teachers and asks us to enter fully into the movement of our learners' lives. We effectively act as mentors when we support, challenge, and provide vision for our learners.

Jane Vella (1994) helps us further understand the qualities of this relationship between the teacher and learner. For Vella, effective teacher-learner relationships are *sound relationships*, "which implies that there is friendship, but no dependency; fun without trivializing the learning; dialogue between men and women who feel themselves peers" (p. 65). Sound relationships reflect:

- Time committed to the relationship
- Affirmation and celebration of the learners' accomplishments
- Mutual respect and the practice of simple courtesies
- Open dialogue

These characteristics are realized through

- Teaching content as open, uncertain, and hypothetical, rather than closed and known with certainty
- Fostering nonjudgmental discussion
- Using open-ended questions in teaching that invite dialogue and discussion, rather than questions for which there are answers at the back of the book
- Engaging in work that learners consider meaningful and significant
- Clarifying roles within the relationship, the boundaries of one's role, and the tasks to be achieved
- Clarifying who is responsible for what
- Providing immediate responses to questions and issues that are raised, which ensures that the learning moment is captured within the experience

Within an ITB approach, the teacher-learner relationship becomes very important to the overall quality of the learning experience. It is probably the component of the instructional process on which all other activities and processes are based. It is hard to overstate the importance of attending to the nature of this relationship and to nurture and sustain the qualities and characteristics discussed in the list continually.

Characteristics of Context-Based Instruction

- Effective instruction actively involves students in determining what they learn and how they learn it.

- Academic skills and subject matter are structured around and integrated with the participating adults' specific contexts and experiences.
- Instructors seek to teach knowledge and skills that are transferable to these real-life contexts.
- Instructors use materials, tasks, and situations characteristic of the worlds their learners inhabit.
- These situations are represented in the ITB approach as "themes."
- Thematic instruction is structured from the concrete (applying for a job) to the abstract (writing effectively and accurately).
- In the ITB approach to instruction, effective teachers are guides on the side rather than sages on the stage.

The learners' social, cultural, and psychosocial contexts are central to ITB instruction. Only when you have a good understanding of these contexts should instruction proceed. More will be said in Chapter Four about how to understand the contexts. In this section, however, we will introduce some general principles about context-based instruction for you to consider as you design and implement experiences for your learners.

Context-based instruction is grounded in the notion that learning should be personally meaningful, relevant, and significant to your learners' lives. One of the ways you can manifest this notion in your instruction is by actively involving learners in determining and shaping what they learn and how they learn it. They will identify problems or issues within their life experiences that, for whatever reason, are really important to them, such as street widening in their neighborhood, unemployment, child care, future educational possibilities, or spousal abuse. We call these contexts "themes."

In context-based instruction, academic skills and subject matter competencies are structured around and integrated within these specific themes. Such skills and competencies are used as a means to learn more about the life issues or problems that have been identified, rather than being learned as ends in themselves. The role of the instructor is to identify the kinds of academic skills and competencies that may be embedded in these various themes and to structure learning experiences so that students can develop these skills while addressing various life themes.

In designing context-based instruction, then, teachers need to consider sequence. In general, learning experiences should be structured so that learners move from small to big, simple to complex, slow to fast (Vella, 1994). This movement is captured in

Figure 3.1.
Kolb Learning Model.

The Kolb learning model provides a useful framework for designing training sessions. While every individual learns best from a particular portion of the process, the most effective learning takes place when all four steps are included in your design. Some portions may not actually take place in the training session itself, but can be brought into the meeting if the students reflect on what they may have experienced in the past or if they plan implementation or application that will take place at the group's next meeting.

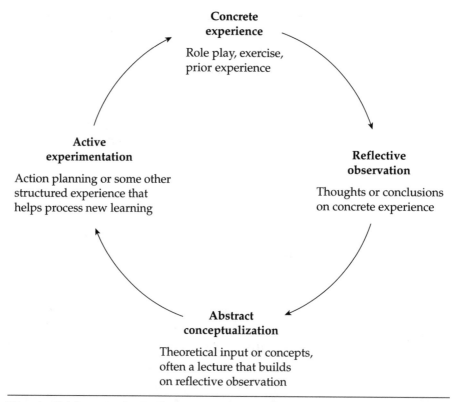

Concrete experience

Role play, exercise, prior experience

Reflective observation

Thoughts or conclusions on concrete experience

Abstract conceptualization

Theoretical input or concepts, often a lecture that builds on reflective observation

Active experimentation

Action planning or some other structured experience that helps process new learning

Kolb's theory of experiential learning (1984), which is illustrated in Figure 3.1. In this theory, learners move from the concrete (specific aspects of the theme) to more abstract learning (e.g., developing competence as a writer or problem solver), and then eventually experimenting with this new level of knowledge.

Let us take the specific example of trying to get a job as a theme around which instruction might be organized. In the *concrete phase*, learners identify, name, and describe concrete experiences that they have had with regard to the theme. They might describe what they have done in the past to get a new or different job. They may even wish to role-play what this was like. In the *reflective phase,* learners engage in activities that ask them to reflect on this theme to elaborate its meaning in their lives. They might describe what it was like for them to go through job-seeking experiences, what seemed to work and what didn't work so well, what parts of the experiences brought about positive emotions and what aspects created negative feelings for them. Additional questions that could be asked include: Who were all the people involved in the various job-seeking experiences? How were they involved? How were the different experiences similar? In what ways were they different? What made them different? The point of this phase of the learning experience is to help learners reach some conclusions as a result of reflecting on the concrete experiences of trying to get a job.

The results of the reflective phase are then used as a base in the *abstract phase.* In this phase, the learner synthesizes the conclusions reached in the reflective phase with more theoretical concepts or material. Teachers can provide information, either through lecture, video, or handouts, on what experts claim to be important characteristics of successful job-seeking efforts. The learners then compare their own findings to the conclusions of the experts and develop a set of principles or guidelines that seem to fit their particular situation of job seeking. In this phase, learners can be encouraged to develop some tentative conclusions about what they might do in the future to deal with similar situations more effectively.

They can try out these ideas or guidelines in the *experimental phase,* either in real or simulated situations. The learners should then evaluate these tryouts to determine what worked and what didn't work, how well they worked, what problems still linger, and how they might be improved in the future.

It should be clear that in this process, the teacher is acting more like a guide than one who holds the wisdom and knowledge. Effective instructors in the ITB approach facilitate the learners' construction of their own knowledge. Thus, it is important for teachers to understand principles of effective facilitation.

Characteristics of Effective Facilitation

- To facilitate adult learning means to go beyond traditional notions of teaching.
- In facilitating, teachers seek to improve the ways individuals and the group address learning tasks. Facilitation is oriented toward process issues and not toward right answers.
- Facilitative teachers guide the learning experience, rather than control and direct it.
- Facilitative teachers encourage collaborative and coopera-

tive methods of inquiry, critical reflection on values, beliefs, and behaviors, and action in response to that learning.

- Effective facilitation makes adults feel more self-directed and empowered.

The term *facilitation* is often used indiscriminately to imply "helping adults learn." Some educators of adults seem especially self-conscious in trying to distinguish what they do from education of children and youth, and referring to their work as facilitation is a way to make this distinction. For some teachers of adults, there seems to be little difference between their "facilitation" and traditional notions of teaching. For others, however, the distinction is more than semantics.

For example, in his book *The Skilled Facilitator* (1994), Roger Schwartz characterizes a facilitator as one who focuses almost exclusively on the group and its processes and dynamics. According to Schwartz, the facilitator is neutral, has no decision-making authority within the group, and intervenes only to help the group improve how it identifies and solves problems and makes decisions. The core values that guide the work of a facilitator are valid information, free and informed choice, and an internal commitment to helping the group make a choice. The facilitator acts solely to improve the effectiveness of the group's processes as it goes about its tasks.

Schwartz's description of facilitators' role helps to distinguish between facilitating and teaching. But educators of adults do not and should not abdicate their authority within the learning setting. Although we encourage educators of adults to be nonjudgmental in their interactions with adult learners, they are seldom able to be neutral. As we describe and characterize the role of facilitation here, it is best to think of what educators of adults do as "facilitative teaching."

When one teaches in a facilitative manner, one places emphasis on democratic and learner-centered approaches. Facilitative teaching underscores the notion of adult learning as collaborative and cooperative and encourages the learner to take responsibility for his or her learning and for the outcomes. In this role, the educator of adults does less controlling and directing of the educational experience and acts more as a guide (Brookfield, 1986; Daloz, 1986). Facilitating adult learning means attending to interpersonal and group process as a means of fostering the learner's sense of self-worth, encouraging collaborative and cooperative methods of learning, stimulating action and reflecting on that action (praxis), fostering critical reflection on the values, beliefs, and behaviors that are part of the cultural and social context of the learner's life and learning, and nurturing self-directed and empowered adults (Brookfield, 1986, pp. 11–12).

The notion of "facilitate" is rooted in the French word *facile*, which means easy. The facilitative teacher makes communicating, planning, problem solving, interacting, having exchanges, and relating easier. The effective facilitator does the job so well that his or her presence is hardly noticed. A leadership role is evident, yet it is not the function of the facilitator to dominate, dictate, engineer, manipulate, undermine, or sabotage the class sessions. Certain roles are simply inconsistent with the aims and values of facilitation (Schwartz, 1994).

The notion of the educator as facilitator provides a framework for fostering participation in the learning group that encompasses a variety of needs and is in tune with the social, psychological, and cultural issues that the learners bring to the group. They may need to point out differences and establish a means of respecting and celebrating those differences. Facilitators do not give the answers, but have a repertoire of possible procedures (called structured activities) that help groups improve the ways in which they go about their learning tasks. Facilitators may point out the direction, a pothole in the road, an easier path, or a dead end, but the effective facilitator will invite the group to decide which way they will proceed in light of that new knowledge.

Usually, the facilitator has the responsibility of coordinating a workshop or class session and attending to the many details that combine to produce a well-organized event or session. Teachers as facilitators may find that one of these details is to remind the learners about the academic competencies that are to be mastered within the topic, if the learners have not already mentioned those skills. It is the role of the facilitator to outline the objectives, purposes, methods, topics, and activities of the class session so participants will know what to expect and what is expected of them. Modifications in the instructional plan are made through a process that obtains the participants' consent and consensus, thereby fostering ownership.

It is also the role of the facilitator to see that all learners actively participate. This might be oral or written participation. It might be participation in a small-group or large-group discussion, or individual feedback given to the facilitator. Effective facilitators ensure that this opportunity is available to learners. The facilitator will also see to it that one person, a few persons, a clique, a group with a vested interest, or the facilitator does not dominate the session.

In group discussion, the facilitative teacher often does not answer questions directly, but instead slides them back to the group to answer. For example, June asks, "Why shouldn't the government have a role in helping us get decent jobs and make a living to support our families?" A facilitator will affirm the importance of the question and then direct it back to the group: "Do any of you have some thoughts about June's question? What should be the role of government in our efforts to get and keep work?" An invigorating discussion on the barriers to jobs that pay a living wage might ensue. Perhaps the group will identify socioeconomic issues involved in getting a job, or maybe they will discuss what jobs are available in the area and the skills required for them. The facilitator will help the group identify these issues and guide them to a realization of how these issues relate to the broader theme they are discussing.

In summary, educators of adults facilitate learning, rather than teach in the traditional sense of imparting information and holding learners accountable for this body of knowledge. In this *Guide*, we distinguish between the role of instructor as facilitator and as the one who controls the learning experience, giving the answers to important questions. An ITB approach to instruction involves facilitative teaching.

Specific Suggestions for Facilitating

To make suggestions for facilitating adult learning, we will first provide a brief case scenario and then will draw from that scenario to highlight how the teacher is implementing the idea of facilitation in the learning settings.

Lisa teaches in a family literacy program in the northeastern part of the United States. There are approximately fifteen women in her program with whom she has been working for several months. Although she spends some of her time each session with the whole group, she also selects activities that allow individuals to work alone, as well as in dyads and other smaller groups. While she is guided by the overall goals and objectives of family literacy as an approach to educating adults, Lisa has fostered a sense of ownership in the group over its learning goals. Each day, someone assigned by the group writes the day's objectives and learning plan on the blackboard so all can clearly see them. Today's goals are stated clearly and specifically so that the learners know what is expected of them. The goals are derived from the theme that has defined the scope of the group's work for the last several days. They reflect the life contexts and situations of the group members.

Prior to today's session, Lisa has double-checked to see that the materials needed for the session are available and ready. She has reviewed the group's last meeting and their assessment of where they needed to go from there. She feels confident about the general guidelines and direction defined by today's session plan, but readily acknowledges to herself the need to be flexible and to respond to particular needs as they might emerge in today's session. As she enters the room this morning, she notes with mild amusement the rows of tables and chairs, left by the accounting night class that shares this classroom space with her. Rolling up her sleeves, she spends several minutes putting them together in the manner most useful for her group and in a way that can be readily changed during the session's work.

The plan for the day involves several kinds of activities, reflecting both the group's theme as well as the goals and objectives of a family literacy program. Today, they will focus on obtaining quality child care for their children—what to look for, how to find potential providers, and how to identify whether they are quality providers. Learners will be asked to describe their previous positive and negative experiences with child care providers. When the class starts, the women share these experiences in small groups, carefully listening to one another's stories. Lisa moves from group to group, gently guiding discussions here and there back to the learning task. She then requests examples that the groups have come up with, and a spokeswoman from each group gives an anecdote shared in her group. Lisa asks each group to identify what made the experiences positive or negative and to list characteristics that they feel reveal desirable and undesirable providers.

Following this task, she distributes a one-page summary of findings from research on early childhood education that talks about effective child care providers. Each member of the group is asked to read the summary to herself and then write down how these findings compare to what the group identified from their own experiences. Then, in the large group, she asks how the research findings are similar to what they identified in their groups and how they are different. "How might you explain why your experiences are somewhat different than those reported in this research?" she asks the group. As questions are raised during the discussion, she paraphrases and directs them back to the group. A vigorous and stimulating discussion ensues over what makes for quality child care and how one can tell whether someone is or is not a good provider. Finally, Lisa asks each learner to describe how they could use this information in looking for their next child care provider. As the groups work, Lisa continues to watch both the clock and the groups, ensuring that they have sufficient time to work but that the pace does not lag, and that all members of the group are engaged with the task in some way.

Teachers should consider the following twelve factors when planning a learning experience using facilitative teaching:

1. *Goals.* Should involve participants and be specific, performance-oriented, and observable so that participants can see the results. Goals must be realistic, attainable, and stated clearly. Lisa involved the group in identifying and maintaining goals for each session, which helped the learners know what was clearly expected of them during that time.

2. *Group size.* Can range from large whole groups to smaller subgroups, triads, pairs, or even one person working alone. Group size must be varied to ensure maximum participation. Lisa's group comprised about fifteen students. Learning groups larger than fifteen begin to suffer in terms of members' opportunities to engage and participate fully in the work of the group. Lisa's group was also large enough that she could effectively work with and move in and out of smaller groups relatively easily.

3. *Time needed.* Must be realistically apportioned to allow for maximum participation and completion of activities. Some groups will insist on taking more time than is realistically available. Occasionally check with participants to see how they feel about the pace of the workshop. Estimating the time needed to complete learning tasks within ITB instruction is not an exact science. Lisa recognized that some tasks might require more time than she had originally planned. Rather than slavishly adhering to her plan, she monitored the group to get a better idea of when to move on to the next task or activity.

4. *Materials.* Make sure you have what you need beforehand in the proper amounts and quantities. Nothing defeats the best laid-out instructional plans like a photocopier that breaks down at the last minute. Lisa prepared her materials well ahead of the group meeting and she could use the premeeting time to check on other things.

5. *Physical setting.* Arrange the furniture and seating plan to suit the particular activity, and rearrange during the session as necessary. It is easy to dismiss the physical arrangement of furniture and other aspects of the learning setting as unimportant, but they do influence the learning process in important and sometimes subtle ways. In ITB instruction, learners need space in which to work (preferably on tables, not individual desks) and they need to be able to move their chairs and adjust their work space freely during the course of the session. Learners need to be able to see each other face-to-face, as well as the instructor. Lisa arrives early enough to ensure that she can rearrange the furniture from the preceding class. As she does so, she thinks about the day's intended activities and what kinds of arrangements will be needed.

6. *Procedures.* Prepare your learning activity. Know your plan and how you hope to accomplish it. Give clear directions so that

participants know what to do. Approach your role with confidence and flexibility, welcoming suggestions and being prepared to make changes to meet the group's needs as the dynamic evolves. Lisa feels comfortable in knowing the group's intended direction for the day, having reviewed that with them the last time they met. A student writes the goals and activities on the board, but Lisa recognizes the need to respond to unanticipated issues that could emerge during the session. The planned activities provide variety, but also connect with the learners' experiences involving the theme in meaningful and important ways.

7. *Sequencing.* Order activities so that they make sense and flow from one to the other. Balance information-giving and listening activities with discussion and internal processing and with breaks and physical activities. In Lisa's group, the learners first focus on their particular and concrete experiences in finding child care providers. From these descriptions, Lisa leads them into more reflective and abstract ways of thinking about the qualities of child care and finally challenges them to use this information as they look for future providers. In this learning task, the learners move from the concrete to the abstract, from the simple to the complex.

8. *Processing information.* Allow time and space for participants to process or discuss the information they are receiving. If people listen without a break, they may feel overwhelmed by all the information. Lisa builds in numerous opportunities for learners to synthesize the information they receive both from each other and from her. These activities allow the learners to integrate this information more fully with their perceptions and experiences of the issue at hand.

9. *Pacing.* Keep things moving to avoid passivity and boredom, but be sensitive to fatigue. Vary the activities from large-group to small-group, from highly passive to physically active, from intensive listening to highly verbalizing, from "I" to "you" to "we" (i.e., change the focus and direction of the talk going on). As a general rule, when things begin to drag, it is probably time to make a change. The different kinds of activities that Lisa uses and the ways in which she monitors the time needed for these activities provide for a comfortable pace to the learning experience. The activities require the learners to read, listen, speak, write, reflect, analyze, and think of ways to apply what they are learning.

10. *Participation.* Try to involve everyone, but allow each to participate as they see fit. Instead of forcing people to speak in turn, allow people to speak at random. Silence is permissible as some people may learn more from watching and listening. While not forcing individuals to participate, Lisa provides small-group activities that allow more timid members to feel more comfortable

talking about their own experiences. She also uses individual work time, so members can express their own thoughts and ideas about the learning task.

11.   *Norms and boundaries.* Participants will quickly set boundaries as to what behavior is allowed and not allowed. Respect these boundaries. If necessary, point out any restrictions, such as smoking, eating, starting times, coffee breaks, asking questions, and so on. Lisa demonstrates her awareness of the importance of working within certain norms and boundaries as she redirects discussions back to the task at hand. In ITB instruction, it is easy for individuals and groups to wander down an infinite number of directions. Often, this happens in the heat of discussion, without the members' being aware that it is happening. It is important for the instructor to reinforce the importance of knowing and adhering to the boundaries of the learning task.

12.   *Using good sense and judgment.* Participants will respect you if you use your good sense and good judgment and are open and forthright with them. For example, if you are not sure of an answer, say so rather than bluffing. Although it is not easy to tell from our case scenario, Lisa demonstrates a strong sense of authenticity in her work with learners. She tends to foster a view of herself as a learner as well as a teacher and sees her students as her teachers. This view is reflected in her relationships with the learners.

Designing and Facilitating for Learning Styles

As we indicated in Chapter Two, learners may differ in how they perceive, remember, think about, and solve learning tasks (cognitive styles); the personal and emotional preferences they express in modes of learning (affective styles); and the preferences they have for environmental and other physical characteristics of the learning environment (physiological styles). Being responsive to these differences and preferences for your students' ways of learning is important to teaching effectively with an ITB approach. In this section, we provide some general suggestions about how you could adapt your instruction to the particular styles your students might manifest. Comprehensive discussion of this issue goes well beyond the scope of this *Guide* and you should not take these brief suggestions as anything more than illustrations of how to address learning styles in the design and implementation of instruction.

Cognitive Differences

One of the easiest differences in cognitive style to observe among learners is in conceptual tempo (Reiff, 1992). This concept refers to a learner's preference to approaching problems in either a rapid or cautious manner, and the level with which they attend to accuracy. Impulsive learners are very curious, respond quickly, take risks, get bored or frustrated easily, and are easily distracted. Reflective learners, on the other hand, want to avoid being wrong or humiliated. They concentrate easily, prefer to work on solitary tasks, and seem more in control of their emotions. Impulsive learners need the learning time and tasks to be broken into smaller segments within a relatively distraction-free environment. Explicit guidelines and directions help them stay focused. They often enjoy role plays and other instructional simulations. Engaging their whole body in the learning is helpful. Reflective learners may need more time on learning tasks and may want time to check their work as well. They are less reluctant to take risks in learning and you may need to model risk-taking behavior to encourage more of its use. Cooperative learning exercises (see Chapter Six) will help reduce some of their anxiety associated with the learning tasks.

Another difference in cognitive style that is commonly and easily observed in adult learning situations is field dependence or independence. Some adult learners seem to learn regardless of the context or "field" in which the learning task is embedded. These field-independent learners tend to be analytical and internally motivated, need less structure and direction, and like to work alone on independent projects. Field-dependent learners are more global in their orientation and attend more to relationships and connections with the learning task. They prefer more structured tasks and working with others in a supportive, cohesive social environment. Field-dependent learners thrive on the collaborative group work so characteristic of ITB instruction, while field-independent learners may quickly become frustrated with lack of progress or clarity. You should vary the learning tasks to ensure that both kinds of learners find their particular preferences supported as well as mildly challenged. Alternating individual assignments with group work, and mixing analytic work and concept-building work will accommodate both kinds of learners.

Affective Differences

Differences in learning associated with personality and emotional characteristics are also relatively easy to identify, especially if you work with the learners over any length of time. One of the most important differences is the way in which learners respond to structure and authority within the learning setting. While some want extensive structure and direction in their learning, others will rebel against what they perceive to be excessive imposition of authority. Respect and respond to these differences, while at the same time using their expression within the learning environment as "teachable moments." Important skills related to interpersonal communication, problem solving, conflict resolution, and negotiation can be nurtured within these situations. You should avoid a tendency to come down on one side or the other of these issues and help the group be aware of both orientations. You can accomplish this by paraphrasing positions that emerge, and then contrasting them with earlier ones, helping the group identify the advantages and disadvantages of both positions.

Differences in conceptual level, which is another way of thinking about affective style, may also present you with some important challenges. Learners at lower levels who have fixed patterns of beliefs and responses or who have difficulty taking another's position should not be made to feel inferior or morally bankrupt. Engaging these learners in narratives and fables, which tend to juxtapose the problems associated with these kinds of thinking with alternative means of approaching problems, often helps individuals see and appreciate the limitations of their current perspectives. Activities have to be devised in which the learners can "live" out vicariously the consequences of their rigid or fixed belief patterns. It may be helpful to engage the higher-conceptual-level thinkers as peer coaches in this form of instruction, in which they work through the various aspects of the story or fable with their fellow students. It should be recognized that conflict between these two groups of learners may sometimes result from the ways in which they perceive problems, rather than the rightness or wrongness of their positions. Focusing the experience on the process of perception rather than a definitive position may be a more effective means to resolution. In general, differences attributed to emotional preferences are seldom responsive to rational and logical kinds of interventions.

Physiological Differences

Preferences for learning based on physiological differences require attention to the physical or environmental characteristics of the learning setting. Wall colors that are light and neutral may be the least intrusive to the learning environment. The room temperature should be kept at a modest level, somewhere between 72 and 76 degrees. Learners that are too warm have few alternatives and can be quite distracted, while learners who may be a little cool can be asked to bring a sweater, jacket, or sweatshirt to the group. Older learners may require more light for tasks involving reading or writing, so it might be helpful to have reading or desk lamps on hand. Some younger learners may prefer video instruction, while other learners may find the noise from this equipment distracting and irritating. Therefore, rooms should be available either for quiet study or for resources that involve more noise. Earphones for computers, video players, or tape recorders can also alleviate this problem without isolating certain learners from the rest of the group. Provide frequent breaks for learners to stretch, get refreshments, or just to visit casually with their peers. If possible, the program should also be offered at different times of the day, especially to accommodate differences in work schedules among the learners.

Gender and Cultural Differences

As we indicated in Chapter Two, some researchers have reported differences in learning that appear to be related to cultural background. These, however, are more difficult to discern readily within a group of adult learners. For example, Chinese students may hold the teacher in high regard, due to traditions within their country, and will sometimes find more constructivist, learner-centered approaches to teaching unfamiliar and strange. For similar reasons, some Middle Eastern students have trouble participating in seminarlike classes, preferring to learn within more teacher-centered and structured environments.

Other cultural differences that have been observed reflect differences in attitudes toward competition and cooperative group work, interpersonal relationships, and other forms of social behavior. Many adult educators who are white and derive from European ancestry have implicit beliefs and values that may, at times, conflict with beliefs and values of learners from other cultures. For example, one of us commented in class one night how difficult it was for him to understand ethnic hatred and warfare and the killing of whole populations based "simply on ethnic differences." Assuming this position to be an obviously humane one, he was surprised to notice an African American woman shaking her head. When he asked her what that meant, she replied, "You won't understand because you are trying to from a white, middle-class, male, American perspective. Some peoples have been fighting each other for centuries and it is a way of life for them." It is thus that our implicit cultural values creep into our teaching in quite benign forms and serve as blinders to a broader understanding of people different from ourselves.

Differences in gender have also been reported in the literature on learning, but these differences are often difficult to discern, especially for white, male teachers. The important issue to address in curriculum and instructional planning is whether the materials and resources adequately represent the positions of different cultures and of women. Racist and sexist stereotypes have been shown to be present in adult literacy material (Quigley & Holsinger, 1993). You should review materials carefully for equity in their treatment of race, gender, religion, and sexual orientation.

To summarize, we have listed some specific suggestions that seem to cut across different styles of learning and represent all phases of the learning cycle:

- Make sure to introduce the group members. Help learners get to know each other.

- Be clear about instructions. Include background information when necessary.

- Do some brainstorming—when addressing specific problems or questions, generate lots of ideas before you narrow things down.

- Make sure to use or apply the data you generate in brainstorming or small-group work to some problem that is meaningful and important to the group.

- Help narrow things down when the time comes. Guide learners through the narrowing-down process, and remember that some learners who like to think in global or divergent ways can be easily distracted from problem solving.

- Provide specific guidance (on how to prioritize, for example).

- Manage time carefully.

- Have participants devise a plan for the work of the session.

- If people get too far off the subject, bring them back. (Learners with a strong need for focus and specific direction will do it for you!) But let people spin out their ideas for a while, too.

- Be creative about some of the assignments or tasks groups will be doing, and be flexible when they get creative on their own!

- Do a lot of problem solving, which is very fun for students with certain kinds of learning styles (e.g., reflective learners).

- Have some parts of each session with clear end products or results.

- Finish each session with a focus on follow-up: for example, what people will do next, or differently, with this information or knowledge.

- Summarize the major messages or learnings from the session at the end.

Characteristics of Collaborative Learning _____

Collaborative learning is fundamental to ITB instruction. What is meant by collaborative learning, however, is not always easy to discern. Educators of adults who want to use collaborative learning must select from a myriad of instructional strategies, such as buzz groups, case study, small-group discussion and investigation, and peer teaching or coaching (Ennis, 1991; Goodsell, Maher, & Tinto, 1992). All of these strategies emphasize different kinds of skills and use varying degrees of structure within the learning experience. For this reason, it is helpful to think of collaborative learning as representing a continuum of learning activities.

This type of learning is a sharp departure from traditional ways of structuring learning in education for adults. Students are no longer passive recipients of information provided by an expert teacher or text. Rather, they are viewed as active agents in constructing knowledge. Collaborative learning provides structured group activities for students and promotes the social skills they need in order to work together. The fundamental principle in collaborative learning is engagement and ownership of learning (Goodsell et al., 1992).

Collaborative learning represents a continuum of learning activities that vary in terms of how much structure is provided, the extent to which the teacher directs the experience, and the complexity of the learning tasks. At one end of this continuum are cooperative learning activities, which are highly structured, teacher-directed, and generally focused on well-defined problems with clear resolutions. At the other end are such approaches as problem-centered learning and learning communities, which are examples of ways to structure learning that cut across disciplines and often stretch out over several months. Students who have relatively little experience in group learning and who are relative novices within the area of study may require strategies that provide more structure. Other learners who are more experienced in both group learning and the subject matter may require less structured activities and minimal supervision. Thus, selection of a particular collaborative strategy depends on what the teacher expects students to learn within the experience and how much support from the teacher students need (Pratt, 1988).

Because of the time-limited nature of many developmental education programs for adults, *cooperative learning* methods are perhaps the most appropriate type of collaborative learning for these settings. This method is also frequently used in integrated or thematic approaches to instruction of adults, and is the approach we use most frequently in this book to illustrate collaborative strategies for fostering adult learning. Cooperative learning methods are usually highly structured and carefully orchestrated by the teacher (Ennis, 1991; Imel, Kerka, & Pritz, 1994; Lane Community College, 1991). Examples include buzz groups, jigsaws, team learning, and round-robin exercises. This approach focuses primarily on having learners master information presented through readings or other resources. Activities and tasks are carefully specified, and learners receive detailed instructions to ensure effective learning experiences. The teacher selects a particular objective, on which the learning task typically focuses, and the teacher often provides information about this objective. The activity may last from a few minutes to several weeks, depending on the context. Most cooperative learning tasks within adult education, however, can be completed within a single meeting.

Cooperative learning strategies stress the interdependence of *all* members, and, through an emphasis on personal accountability and responsibility, activities are designed so that each member contributes. Roles, such as the group recorder, reporter, and so forth, are often carefully assigned and explained. The tasks assigned are relatively unambiguous, circumscribed in scope, and addressed within distinct time frames. This form of collaborative learning helps learners consolidate their understanding of lecture material, master specific factual information from readings, solve multistep problems in various subject matters, and relate individual experiences to the topic at hand. Problem-solving, interpersonal, and teamwork skills are also developed through participation in cooperative learning activities (Hart-Landsberg & Reder, 1993; McLaughlin, 1993).

The specific strategies and techniques of cooperative learning will be discussed in Chapter Six. In general, however, cooperative learning is characterized by five key elements:

- Learners are interdependent. They need to depend on one another to succeed in the learning task.

- Each member is held responsible and accountable for a particular part of the learning task. The teacher assesses learning and gives results back to the group so that all learners know who needs help in what area.

- Groups of learners evaluate how well they are doing on the learning task, taking note of what was done well and what could be improved.

- Learning requires students to use a variety of social skills, including leadership, decision making, trust building, conflict management, conflict resolution, encouraging, listening, and giving feedback.

- Learning takes place through face-to-face interaction, as students verbally discuss various aspects of the learning task.

In addition, other small-group activities are also helpful in adult developmental education. These include small-group discussion (Imel et al., 1994) and teamwork (Hart-Landsberg & Reder, 1993). In general, these activities are less structured and more open-ended. They give learners a forum to express and explore their own beliefs and values about particular topics. They provide an excellent means of fostering process skills, such as active listening and other interpersonal skills, reflective and critical thinking, and problem solving. These less structured activities are more challenging for the instructor to facilitate effectively, but foster personal growth and learning in powerful ways (Brookfield, 1986).

Thus, if you are considering the use of collaborative learning strategies, you face a wide array of possible approaches. If you select a particular approach, it should reflect the overall aims of the instructional process, the kinds of knowledge and skills being developed, the skills, willingness, and readiness of the learners, and the overall context in which the learning is taking place.

Summary

In this chapter, we have covered several instructional issues that are important components of ITB instruction. These are the teacher-learner relationship, context-based instruction, facilitative teaching, taking differences in the way adults learn into account, and collaborative learning. In addition to providing what we consider to be some of the more important characteristics of these various components, we also listed the implications that these components hold for providing ITB instruction.

CHAPTER 4

Identifying, Selecting, and Planning Theme Units

A thematic approach to curriculum and instruction is a way of connecting the learner's life experiences in a relevant and meaningful way to academic skills and competencies, such as reading, writing, and computing, and to process skills, such as critical thinking, problem solving, communicating, negotiating, and working in a team. The thematic approach recognizes that learning involves a complex interweaving of life experiences and skills. It represents a multilayered approach to facilitating learning and involves simultaneous application of multiple disciplines. Rather than stressing the unique characteristics of different subject matters, the thematic approach emphasizes connections among these disciplines, especially when it comes to particular life issues.

The Nature of Themes

Theme units are ways of integrating a variety of knowledge and skills around a particular idea or issue. These units represent quite a different way of thinking about what one teaches. They contrast with more focused approaches (see Chapter One), in which concepts, goals, and instructional activities are designed to address a particular discipline. Selecting the task of writing a business letter and then incorporating the skills of language arts in this task is an example of a focused approach.

In a broad sense, themes can be represented in several different ways. For example, some of the teachers we observed organized their instruction around geographic themes, such as the Caribbean, because the majority of their students or their students' families were from that area. Others chose current political topics such as the environment to integrate science, language arts, social studies, and math. The teacher who implemented an integrated program of reading within the correctional facility organized the curriculum around a study of the natural world. These examples illustrate the use of themes that focus on general topics or ideas important to the learners.

While these teacher-selected, topical themes provide helpful contexts for integrating academic competencies within the study of a particular topic, they tend to be removed from or more abstract than the learners' immediate life situations. They also run the risk of implicitly embodying unhelpful and even destructive stereotypes of adult learners as deficient or in desperate need. For example, the topical theme of "abusive relationships" may convey a picture of participants in these programs as abusive or abusing persons (Quigley, 1997). Grounding theme selection more in learners' lives helps guard against such use of stereotypes.

In this *Guide,* themes are seen as an integral part of contextual learning (Chapter Two). We believe teachers should select themes, preferably with direct learner involvement, from learners' personal, work, or community contexts. Several of the teachers in our project also reflected this interpretation of theme-based instruction, particularly an ESL teacher and an instructor in a family literacy program. Although they were able to involve their learners directly in identifying and selecting themes to varying degrees, the teachers used themes that represented their learners' particular life contexts. Our use of the notion of theme is consistent with this perspective.

Themes represent aspects of the learners' lives that have particular immediacy or salience, but are broader in scope and application than specific questions or problems that may need answers. Themes often capture a variety of social, cultural, political, and economic issues in which the lives of the participating learners are inextricably interwoven. The themes represent interrelated clusters of problems, issues, or concerns (life skills) that the learners face. These units recognize what learners already know within these contexts and seek to build on these strengths. The workplace, job training, family, and the community are all broad contexts within which themes may be identified. Getting into college, working with landlords, getting a job, finding and providing quality child care, and dealing with governmental agencies are examples of themes that could emerge in developmental education programs for adults.

Academic competencies such as reading, writing, and math skills, as well as process skills like problem solving, critical thinking, learning-to-learn, and interpersonal skills, are all integrated in the study of a single theme. Academic and process skills are used to learn more about this problem or concern. What students bring to the learning setting determines where learning begins (Shor, 1992).

For example, Larry, the learner discussed in Chapter Two, brought with him an interest in and knowledge of mechanics and the tools used in this work context. Although he did not think of his work context as relevant to his present learning tasks, the volunteer tutor helped him see the connections between mixed fractions and the calibrations of socket wrenches. When the learning task began with this context, Larry could make sense of content that otherwise had no meaning for him. He could see that what he was doing had relevance to a personal situation.

Materials used to teach basic skills reflect the personal, work, or community contexts within which learners will use these skills. For Jake and his colleagues enrolled in the corrections reading program discussed in Chapter Two, reading came alive when the instructor began organizing the curriculum around the students' interest in the natural world. The instructor selected materials that represented or addressed that theme. Printed material from NASA, workbooks focusing on the study of science, and videotapes from *National Geographic* provided materials that fostered both the students' competence in reading and that furthered their understanding of the natural world. These materials were supplemented with hands-on laboratory experiments, which also required the students to read before they could set up the experiments and interpret the results. Reading, indeed, became a way for the students to learn.

The last example demonstrates that themes need not always be specific problems or issues that learners face in their lives. In this project, learning was structured around a generative idea, that is, an idea that the learners found meaningful, relevant, and exciting. Generative ideas represent another powerful approach to integrating instruction (Prawat, 1991).

Why Use a Thematic Approach?

The rationale for using a theme-based approach in educating adults was addressed in the Preface and Chapter One. Before discussing ways to identify and select themes, we provide a summary of this rationale. Theme-based instruction:

- Makes the student the center of the curriculum.

- Makes the content directly relevant to the learner.

- Uses words that have special power and meaning to the learner.

- Uses written vocabulary and syntax that are part of the learner's vocabulary and language pattern, clearly illustrating the link between spoken and written English.

- Provides for the creation of a "dialogical" relationship where the student and teacher become colearners and are both actively and creatively involved.

- Treats the learners and their experiences with respect.

- Results in greater and more immediate success.

- Allows students to articulate and confront insecurities about learning and their lives.

- Provides learners with an approach and environment different from that which they associate with their unsuccessful school experiences.

- Produces compelling and original readings at the learner's appropriate language level.

- Allows students and teachers to place primary attention on communication and self-expression rather than on phonics.

The advantages of using a contextually grounded, theme-based approach when instructing adults are discussed more fully in other publications, as well (e.g., Auerbach, 1992; Kovalik, 1993; Ministry of Advanced Education and Job Training, 1987; Shor, 1992).

Selecting Themes

Selecting themes means identifying what content the students will study. An exemplary teacher in our project who uses ITB instruction described her approach as "a giant amoeba. . . . It begins and keeps moving and spreading and involving new things. It's one big, hungry monster." The image of the hungry monster or amoeba that reaches out, oozing over many topics and issues, reminds us that themes are alive and relevant to our learners. One teacher asked, "When does context stop? There is so much to keep discovering!" Of course, the answer is that the life context of the learner provides limitless opportunity for themes, topics, and learning opportunities.

There are many ways to approach this amoeba. In considering a contextual or integrated approach, teachers may feel more comfortable beginning with the basic math, reading, and writing skills that need to be developed, and then designing learning activities that students will apply in the functional context. This is the focused approach that was discussed in Chapter One. For example, if students need basic reading and addition skills, one could have them read want ads and calculate costs of rent and utilities, which they can then apply to their search for housing. The problem with this approach is that it starts with the academic skill, rather than the learners' life experiences.

This *Guide* suggests that you start with the life context of the learners and the particular life skill they need. For example, Omar needs to find affordable housing. The life skills he needs may include filling out forms, preparing a budget, identifying references, and so forth. From this needed life skill, you will identify vocabulary, problem-solving strategies, math skills, and reading-for-content skills that Omar needs. Your learning activities will derive from the life context identified and the life skill needed.

One teacher reported that this approach "liberated" her from having to think up ideas. "It's amazing," she said. "We have no shortage of ideas. If anything, we won't ever run out." Careful selection of themes will provide success and will empower learners to apply their skills to new areas. One word of caution—the hungry monster can provide such a long laundry list of things to work on that learners may quickly become disillusioned or disempowered. Take care to help learners prioritize the themes and activities.

The process of identifying, selecting, and prioritizing themes, and designing a curriculum around them, is the focus of this section. It is important for teachers to remember, however, that curriculum design in the ITB approach partly relies on an emergent perspective. That is, through posing problems and doing other activities to generate ideas for themes, learners actively participate in designing the curriculum. This process is not to be viewed as a precursor to instruction. As the learners engage in identifying and selecting themes, there will be numerous opportunities to foster important process and academic skills, such as reading, language arts, interpersonal communication, teamwork, and negotiation. Teachers should enter the theme-planning phase of instruction aware of these opportunities and should plan instructional activities that identify and reinforce these skills.

Thematic instruction is most effective when themes are selected as a result of negotiation and teamwork among the students. Because of the nature of some learning settings, however, such a process may not always be feasible. Programmatic constraints, such as time allowed for the program, learners' schedules, enrollment policies, and meeting times may make a learner-generated approach to theme selection difficult to implement in an effective manner. Thus, teachers may sometimes need to select themes for the learners (Shor, 1992), with considerable attention to and focus on the learners' particular contexts and life experiences. Regardless of the process used or who selects the themes, they should be interesting to students and should reflect content that students value outside the learning setting. In Shor's words, the themes should "be their words, understanding, self-respect, and desire to learn more" (p. 37).

The Process of Theme Selection

Auerbach and Wallerstein (1987, quoted in Shor, 1992) identify three basic steps of the theme selection process: (1) listening to students to learn about their issues and life contexts; (2) speaking to students about these themes; and (3) figuring out ways to act on the problems identified in the themes. The ABLE Network expands on these three steps by suggesting ways teachers can select themes:

- Use formal and informal classroom discussion to help identify and develop topics of interest. In these discussions, topics frequently emerge that can then become issues that students would like to explore further.
- Use questions such as: "What really bothers you these days?"; "What are you most worried or concerned about?"
- Use photographs or pictures from newspapers or magazines. Select these pictures with the learners' community, work, and family contexts in mind.

  Present the pictures to a small group of learners or to individual learners.

  Ask them to select a picture that they feel strongly about.

  Discuss with the whole group what the pictures represent to them. Record the students' responses. You can often identify themes by examining these responses.

- Use articles with large headlines from current newspapers or magazines.

  Ask students to read the headlines and discuss what the headlines mean to them.

  Record the students' responses to the headlines. Identify themes by examining these responses.

In the first phase of theme selection, the teacher and students are trying to identify ideas or topics around which to organize the curriculum. It is not recommended that the teacher ask the students what they would like to learn. In discussing the first step in a dialogical approach to teaching, Vella (1994) talks about how she did a "needs assessment" for a "train-the-trainer" program in the midst of the 1984 Ethiopian famine. Her learners were a group of young people who had agreed to work as trainers in the relief program. They had little job experience and no experience as teachers or trainers. What should their training program focus on? Vella recalls:

> As a diagnostic task I invited them to draw a map of the area, putting in all the vital information they thought I should know. I learned that they did know a great deal about the people of Epheson (the town) and less about those in the mountain villages. . . . I learned that we had two artists in the group. . . . I watched who made decisions about what information should go on the rough map. . . . As their replies [to questions] were translated, and I documented them, I learned a bit about each person's value system. . . . I discovered that these sixteen youth were literate and numerate, knew Ethiopian history, and felt deeply about the drought and the need for their country to become self-reliant. They understood that the ravaging of trees from the mountains to provide firewood and charcoal for the growing urban population had caused this drought. . . . Since they were semi-urban youth from towns along a main road, they had much to learn from rural Ethiopians (pp. 48–50).

The process Vella used generated much information about her learners, showing what they already knew and what they would need to know to work effectively as trainers in the relief program. "Imagine," she says, "what would have happened if I had asked this group directly . . . what they thought they needed to learn. Such an approach to needs assessment would have resulted in nothing authentic or useful" (p. 50). By using the map as a generative symbol, by asking open-ended questions, and by stimulating dialogue among all the participants, Vella assessed the learning needs in a natural and spontaneous way.

The suggestions provided above reflect this approach to identifying learning themes within developmental education programs for adults. Through the use of visual stimuli, such as pictures or photographs, learners will tell their stories and describe salient life contexts. When they convey these narratives within a safe atmosphere of discussion and open-ended questions, they can generate considerable information that will serve as the basis for forming themes.

A brief case example will help illustrate how this process of theme selection worked in a group of young adult learners. This group consisted of young parents or soon-to-be parents who were out of school. Some of them worked in various jobs, but some were not employed. They were clients of a family practice clinic that provided their medical care, and all were confronted with caring for a newborn baby. In the initial meeting, the educator led the group in an open-ended discussion about the area they all shared—what it was like to be a new or soon-to-be parent. The educator distributed articles from the local newspaper about parenting, teenage pregnancies, and the potential job market for young people, and several members of the group commented on the headlines. The educator asked the group members which of the articles or headlines they felt most strongly about. While the learners talked, the educator took careful notes about what ideas or topics seemed to generate high levels of emotion and interest. The learners expressed numerous ideas and opinions in this discussion, which began to cluster around broader topics. Among the themes identified were: "caring for my child," "getting and maintaining adequate medical care," "finding a good job," "rebuilding relationships with my family," and "dealing with government agencies."

As is evident from this brief example, these procedures can generate several possible themes from which the students and teacher will need to select. They can use a number of activities to accomplish this final selection:

- Have the learners vote on a theme.

    Write the possible themes on the board or a flip chart.

    Instruct the group that they need to decide on a theme to study.

    Individuals vote on the theme they feel is the most interesting.

- Have the learners rate the themes.

    Record the possible themes on newsprint or a flip chart.

    Give each student five colored dots.

    Students use the dots to show which themes they are most interested in. They can spread their dots over several themes or use all of them on one theme.

    The theme with the most dots will be selected for study.

- Use criteria to select themes that remain generative and vital for the students. For example, the following criteria can be used for selecting reading materials for adult literacy students:

    The material must be meaningful to the student.

    The reading material must be complete.

    The reading material must have literary merit.

The material must be available.

The material must be inexpensive.

The reading material must "promote the integration of our students' developed language abilities—their memory and conversational skills—with developing language."

- The students may wish to come up with their own criteria, which you can then use to rate and select themes to use for study.

The learners in the case example about soon-to-be parents chose to rate the themes they had identified. On a flip chart, the teacher listed each of the themes generated in the group discussion. The students each received five colored dots and were told to place a dot by each theme that interested them the most and that they wanted to focus on in their learning experience. The teacher carefully explained that, in this rating process, they could spread their dots out over five different themes, could use them all on one theme, or could put any number of dots on any theme they wanted to study. The students eagerly took to the flip chart, chatting with each other about their preferences, and watching as the rating process unfolded. When it was over, the theme of "caring for my child" had the largest number of dots, followed by "finding a good job." The learners had just selected a theme around which their instructional program would be initiated. The teacher felt satisfied that this theme provided an ample basis for integrating the wide variety of academic, life, and process skills that would be taught in the program. Most importantly, it was a theme of utmost salience to the participating learners.

Assessing Theme Effectiveness

Susan Kovalik (1993), author of *ITI The Model: Integrated Thematic Instruction*, says that curriculum is highly personal and very intellectually challenging. We often find that our best plans do not work and that surprising approaches click with our students. How do you know that a theme is working? What criteria should you use for evaluating a theme? We suggest that you ask yourself the following questions as part of the evaluation process:

- Are your students excited about the theme?
- Are you excited about it?
- Is the conceptual idea underlying the theme and the related content meaningful from your student's point of view?

- Does the theme sufficiently support and enrich the learning objectives of the course or program?
- Does the theme have substantive application to the real world?
- Did your learners participate in selecting the theme? Or did they express an interest in pursuing this theme?
- Is the rationale behind the theme truly compelling for you and your students? Or are you stretching the link between your students and an issue?
- Is the theme appropriate for your learners' age and experience?
- Are resources readily available?

As the group settles back from this prioritizing exercise, it is a good time for the teacher to make observations about the themes, guided by these criteria. Let us use the young parents group as a way of illustrating how a teacher might use this list to assess the themes identified and selected. The two themes with the highest ratings in this group were "caring for my child" and "finding a good job." During the preliminary discussions, as well as the rating process, the teacher observed that these themes generated high levels of participation and interest, particularly "caring for my child." The learners talked a lot about this issue, their voices often elevated and animated as they exchanged stories and experiences about their new or impending roles as parents. These impromptu discussions were occasionally punctuated with brief, heated exchanges and disagreements. The room was filled with noise and excitement during the rating process and as the results became evident, no one objected to the dominance of the theme. Several learners nodded in agreement as the teacher summarized the results of the rating. The teacher found herself swept up in the learners' excitement and silently acknowledged the wisdom of the learners' choice. "Becoming a parent," she told the group, "is one of the toughest learning assignments there is and you have challenged yourself by recognizing its importance for you."

As the learners rated the themes, she evaluated them herself. They all had clear applications to the real-world contexts of these learners, but some themes seemed more immediate than others. "Caring for my child" and "finding a good job" were challenges that were right around the corner for these learners. Furthermore, it was apparent that these themes would provide a substantive basis for bringing in a number of academic and life skills as well. Questions generated by these themes had no easy or straightforward answers, and the students would be engaged in doing research and applying problem-solving and critical thinking skills to what was found out through this research. Their reading and writing abilities would be strengthened, and they would need to use a number of mathematical skills in planning a family budget. The teacher felt confident that the themes represented important aspects of these learners' life contexts, and that they encompassed a wide variety of the academic and life skills that these learners would need as they embraced their new roles as parents.

But would they have sufficient materials and resources to address these themes? Parenting is not an issue that has received much attention in traditional developmental education programs for adults. The teacher, however, was cooperating with the family practice clinic in this program. One of the goals of this clinic was to provide parenting education through their medical services. She felt confident that the clinic would have a variety of print, video, and audio resources for the learners to use. In addition to the clinic, several community-based agencies were available, including the high school and the YWCA, that provided a variety of services to young new parents. She concluded that the themes met the requirements, and she agreed that they were ready to begin organizing a course of study around the themes.

How to Structure and Use a Theme Unit

Let us assume that you and your students have tentatively identified a theme that you can use as a focus for a unit of instruction. We will call this a "theme unit." At the risk of imposing too much structure on this process, we have created a form that we believe will be helpful in designing instruction using this approach. This form and its underlying processes may be especially helpful for new teachers or for those with little or no background in this approach to instruction. It is our intention that this form be used as a guide in a way that will help you integrate academic competencies and process skills with the study of the life issues reflected in this theme. An example of this form is provided in Exhibit 4.1.

In the upper, right-hand box, write the name of the theme that has been identified. In the box to the immediate left of this area, record some of the relevant life experiences that have been named within the context of this theme. Together, you and your learners can explain what could or should be learned about this theme. Write this information in the space "Forming objectives."

As you begin to design or select possible instructional strategies, keep in mind your intended academic competencies (e.g., reading, writing, and math); the process skills of problem solving,

Exhibit 4.1.
   Instructions for Sample Theme Units.

Life experience	**Theme**
This may be in the form of a quote and will be generated from the learners.	This is the topic to be covered.

Forming objectives

Ask your learners how to respond to the life experience issue and what can be done about it. Ask what they would like to learn about the issue (the objectives). Add your opinion.

Sample objectives	**Strategies**
These are written in precise, measurable terms which describe what the learner will accomplish.	These are written to focus on the learner's activities—what the teacher will have the learner actually do. As you debrief each strategy you may find that it leads to a new activity or strategy or to the development of new objectives.

Skills developed

Identify the concrete competency or life skill to be accomplished: reading, math, writing, critical thinking, learning to learn, or problem solving. This can serve as a checklist for skills that are not acquired. You might alter a strategy to accomplish a new skill.

Formats used

Write down the format used with each strategy. You may find you rely on lecture too often. Try a new approach and vary the instructional setting.

learning-to-learn, and critical thinking; and interpersonal skills. The formats and strategies (see Chapter Six) selected should directly address the life experiences reflected in the theme, but should also be chosen to maximize the opportunity to work on these sets of skills as well. Formats refer to the kind of learning experience intended, such as whole-group, small-group, or individual work, or work within the community. Strategies refer to the specific activities you are planning within these formats. For example, you may decide that, for a given theme, individual, small-group, and community formats are appropriate. Then, within each of these formats, you may find it helpful to specify which activities would address the issues that the learners raised in this area. You should list these strategies in the appropriate space on the form.

As you start identifying and naming specific strategies, list in the space called "Skills developed" the academic competencies to be addressed and the process and interpersonal skills to be practiced. List significant vocabulary words that the students may encounter in the study of this theme. After this, you may find it helpful to list objectives or outcomes for the session in the box labeled "Sample objectives." Finally, identify the educational resources you will need to implement this unit and any community resources that may be relevant. Record these on the back of the form.

This form provides a way of structuring and organizing one's thinking and planning for ITB units. As teachers become more comfortable and more experienced with this method, it is likely they will rely on the form less, attending intuitively to the needs presented by this approach. For those who are not familiar with ITB teaching, however, the form should present a comfortable starting place.

Implementing ITB Instruction: A Way to Begin

As you begin to work with the ITB approach to instructing adults, you will undoubtedly develop a model of implementation that is appropriate for you, your learners, and your practice setting. We have, however, found one model especially helpful in laying out a conceptual overview of how to approach and implement a theme unit. This model is illustrated in Figures 4.1 and 4.2. It was developed by the ABLE Network and is commonly referred to as the *I*CANS* model. This model represents a more detailed description of the instructional process briefly described in Chapter Three. Figure 4.1 gives a conceptual overview of theme-based instruction, and Figure 4.2 provides a more detailed description of each of the phases of the process. On the far left of Figure 4.2, the academic

Figure 4.1.
Theme Cycle.

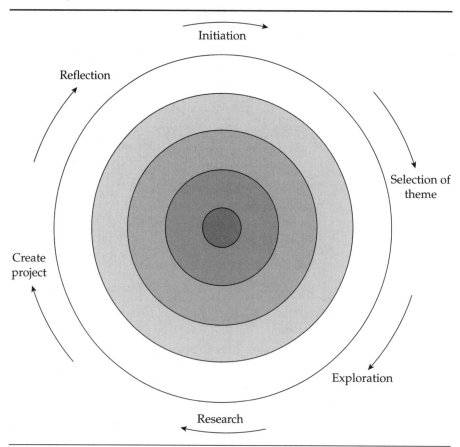

Source: Reprinted with permission from the *I*CANS* Project, Washington State Board for Community & Technical Colleges.

competencies are identified as being addressed throughout the theme process. On the far right, the model identifies the specific process skills, which are reflected in the various steps or phases of the instructional process. Listed under the column called "Process," these steps specify the general instructional tasks that you as a facilitator of learning must face as you implement this approach. These steps are spelled out in a little more detail under the column labeled "Description." This part of the model specifies the kinds of questions addressed in each of the instructional phases.

While it is not necessary that every theme unit follow the sequence of activities listed in Figure 4.1, the model does provide a useful point of departure for thinking about the specifics of the instructional process. It also clearly communicates the multilayered nature of the ITB approach. Virtually any instructional activity is a site for learning at multiple levels and dimensions.

In the case of the group of young and expectant parents, the teacher already moved them through the processes of initiation and theme selection. As she did so, she kept in mind the objectives for these two processes (listed under "Description" in Figure 4.2). In addition, she sought to foster work on the life skills (listed under "Workplace Skills") and academic competencies (far left of Figure 4.2) possible in these phases. As her students begin working with the theme, they will explore what they already know about it, so that the instructional process can build on these prior experiences. Jane Vella's work with the young trainers (described earlier), exemplifies how exploration of what is already known can also be woven into the needs assessment or theme selection process. From there, the teacher will help frame the specific questions they want to research and how they can go about addressing them. This phase of the process involves gathering and mastering information, practicing specific skills, and so forth.

The learning process is strengthened when it is augmented with some kind of application. In the "Create project" phase, the learners seek to use what they have learned within the context of a particular project. In the case of the parent group, this may mean making sure their home has been "baby proofed," checking out different formulas in the grocery stores, comparing prices and nutritional contents, or doing a practice run of going to the hospital emergency room in case the need for urgent medical care arises.

The reflection phase of the instructional process involves looking both back and forward. Together, the learners and teacher look back on their work around the selected themes. They will review specific questions or problems that emerged to determine whether they have been effectively addressed. They will also review the methods and approaches used to learn about these issues, and try to identify both the strengths and weaknesses of these processes. The reflection phase will also involve looking forward to how the knowledge and skills acquired might be useful in future situations.

For example, the members of the teen parents group would reflect back on their work around the theme of "Caring for my child." They would examine the processes used to select the theme, as well as techniques for further exploration. They may discover that the processes worked quite well. But they may also learn, for example, that not all of the members were equally heard, or that they had rushed a critical decision. They will want to identify "missed opportunities," in which the group could have learned more about particular skills or knowledge related to the theme. They will also ask what situations are similar to caring for a baby to identify other areas in which the body of knowledge and skill can be applied.

Figure 4.2.
I*CANS* Themes.

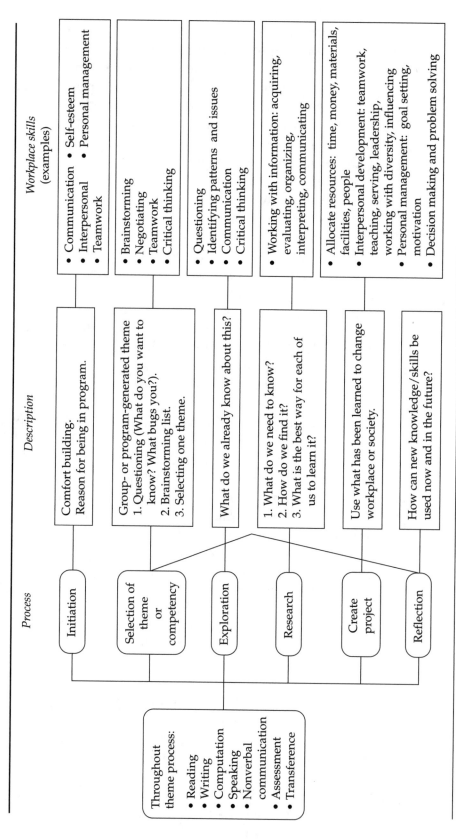

Source: Reprinted with permission from the *I**CANS* Project, Washington State Board for Community & Technical Colleges. Originally provided by Shash Woods and Bill Sperling, Adult Basic Literacy Educators Network, n.d.

As teachers begin to implement ITB instruction, they should devote a small part of their total instructional time to using the *I*CANS* model and can expand it as they and the learners become increasingly comfortable with its philosophy and procedures. The class may not always use the process illustrated in Figures 4.1 and 4.2. For certain groups working on certain themes, different parts of the model may need to be emphasized more than others. We encourage teachers to relax into the process and have fun with their learners as they explore this different way of teaching and learning together.

Questions Teachers Ask About an ITB Approach

We know that teachers will have doubts, concerns, or maybe even insecurities shifting to an ITB approach. Using this approach is difficult to describe. Here are some frequently asked questions about this approach and some responses.

• *How will I know a theme when I see one?* A theme among a group of learners is apparent when an idea or topic seems to take off within the group and they get really excited and interested in talking about it. Their involvement engenders an intense self-directedness within the group. Themes engender feelings and emotions, as well as content, about particular issues in learners' lives.

• *How can I tease out a theme from my group? They are very shy with each other.* You may want to set the tone with some start-up activities that help the group get to know each other. Similar to Jane Vella's use of the map, this may include drawing a "river of life," where the group members draw the events in their lives, identifying tributaries or changes in the course of their lives (see Figure 4.3 for an example). Use big pieces of butcher paper and crayons. Using the metaphor of a river as their life's journey, ask the students to think about the experiences and issues that have shaped them, about key events in their life and key people who have influenced them. The events and people can be positive or negative influences. The important thing is that they have had an impact.

Ask the students to think of themselves at three different points in their life history: in the past, right now, and in the future. Have them draw that history in the shape of a river flowing through time. Ask them to describe the currents that have shaped them, the rapids they have overcome, the meandering streams where they went off in new or different directions. Have them think about now. What does it look like? Which elements are part of their lives now? Finally, if there is time, ask them to consider

Figure 4.3.
   Sample River of Life.

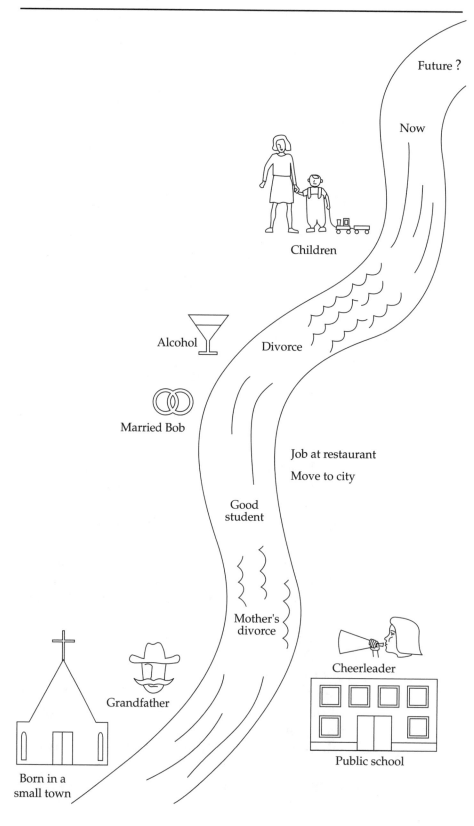

their future and to draw what it might look like. (Note: we often do this as a separate goal-setting and planning exercise.)

Allow plenty of time (fifteen to twenty minutes) for the drawing. Reassure your students that stick people are fine and that they may use symbols. Encourage them to work quietly and reflectively. The instructions should be purposely vague in that you do not want to tell them what to draw. You want their images to come out and their creativity to flow.

Ask the students to share their drawings with the class and to tell their story. While this will take some time, it will set the stage for further interaction among the students. From this you can begin to know the context of learners and to identify possibly emergent themes. You might ask them to share what was hard about coming to class today. This is a particularly good question when the group appears distracted. Encourage them to see concerns or experiences that they share with others.

• *I don't have time to cover all the material as it is. I certainly don't have time to spend on group process.* To reiterate what we have said several times, adults learn best when their learning is grounded in the contexts and situations of their life experiences (Brookfield, 1986; Daloz, 1986; Freire, 1970; Jarvis, 1992; Merriam & Caffarella, 1991; Shor, 1992). For adults, content is not an end in itself, but a means to addressing other ends, problems, questions, issues, or interests that arise within the day-to-dayness of their lives.

To develop an instructional program that responds to this way of learning, we have to learn to listen to our students (Vella, 1994). Attend to group process as a major component of the educational experience. If you work wisely with the group, they will help you better identify the content that needs to be covered. You may not end up using any more time than you do now, or it may be that the time you and the learners do spend on content is more effective because they are getting more out of it. In addition, participation in group activities provides learners with opportunities to practice a host of skills they will need to be effective in their work, families, and communities.

• *It sounds like you can't do any planning. What if my lesson plans are derailed by an issue that the group or individual brings up? What if they do not agree on a focus?* On the contrary, this approach requires considerable planning. We like to call it planning at several layers. The difference is that you are planning within the context of learners' experiences.

For example, say you have promised to spend an hour reviewing basic math skills that will be on the GED exam and Diana arrives with a concern that her food stamps were cut. She is upset and wants to discuss this with the group. You may want to negotiate the class agenda with the group. Or you might suggest to the group that they discuss Diana's story for a set period of time and remind them of the need to go over the math. The issue here is that you negotiate the time and assure Diana that her concern will be met.

•   *What are some of the constraints on this process?* Teachers and facilitators of adult learning say that one of the major downsides to this approach is that they lack sufficient planning time. Many instructors are paid only for contact time. To employ this approach most effectively, instructors will need institutional support for planning.

Summary

In this chapter, we discussed what is meant by "themes" and the various ways in which one can conceptualize or think about themes for instructional planning. We summarized several key advantages of a theme-based approach and discussed the process of identifying and selecting particular themes within learning settings. The chapter explored ideas about how to generate themes, prioritize them, and select one from several that the group may have identified. We also discussed the importance of monitoring a particular theme's effectiveness and suggested ways in which that could be accomplished. We presented a planning form that may help teachers structure units around student themes. Finally, we presented a model from the ABLE Network that conceptualizes the instructional process itself, from convening as a group of learners to testing the knowledge derived through the learning process in some kind of concrete, experiential project. As a way of pulling all this information together, we briefly addressed the questions teachers ask.

CHAPTER 5

Sample Theme Units

This chapter contains sample theme units that we hope will spark the creativity of teachers and facilitators of adult learning. We will take you through our process step by step and, in doing so, hope that you will gain a feel for the process of developing a theme. Our units are by no means exhaustive. Indeed, there is room for many new ideas. Skilled teachers may not need this structure and might find these units too detailed, too limiting, or unnecessary. Some may find that our charts contradict our idea of the spinning top, which evokes an ongoing process. Yet facilitators of adult learning who are new to this approach may appreciate the guidance. The units relate to traditional curricular planning and offer examples of the process of theme development. We do not intend for these sample units to substitute for your process of theme development, but rather to provide a guide.

Exhibits 5.1 through 5.5 demonstrate theme units developed in concrete settings of practice. We will use the example in Exhibit 5.1 to illustrate the key tasks in the process of developing a theme unit. (The blank form in Exhibit 5.5 can also serve as a checklist for the teachers as they go through the process.)

1. *Listening to your learners.* As we have stated earlier, themes must arise out of the learners' life experience. Through a formal or informal process of listening to the learners, the facilitator will identify key concerns. This may be in the form of a quote, as in our examples, or a list of issues that your learners have brought to the table. In the discussions with learners, note the universality of the concerns and concepts that arise.

2. *Naming the theme.* A theme is a universal concept that will help facilitate study of the academic competencies the students must master. As you state the theme, grounding it in the learners' concerns, be sure to do so in a fashion that has broad appeal and reflects the universal nature of the concept. Everyone in the class should be able to relate to the theme in some fashion.

3. *Forming objectives.* We recommend that teachers develop a process for forming objectives with their students so as to increase student involvement in the theme. This can be accomplished through simple brainstorming or goal-setting exercises. Many facilitators develop the objectives themselves due to time constraints. We strongly suggest that this step not be eliminated, as group ownership in the activities may increase participation and interest.

4. *Writing objectives.* After identifying the students' learning objectives, state them in measurable, specific, and achievable language. This step is also a prelude to the assessment step, so facilitators should be thinking about how to assess mastery of content or skills.

5. *Developing strategies.* Identify several strategies for each of the objectives. Ask the students for their ideas as well. This step provides an excellent opportunity for the adult learners to develop activities that they can apply directly to their own lives. The strategies may change as new ideas emerge from the group and as you evaluate students' mastery of the content. Step 5 goes hand-in-hand with step 6, as you will want to vary activities to increase students' mastery of adult developmental skills.

6. *Reviewing the skills.* You should review the academic and process skills used in the lesson plan and alter the activities to assure that students practice a variety of skills. This is an important step to share with the learners as a review of what they have accomplished in the theme unit.

7. *Reviewing instructional formats.* This is a quick checklist for the teacher to determine if he or she has attempted a variety of formats or is too dependent on one or two instructional formats. As discussed earlier, adult learners vary in their comfort levels and a variety of formats will provide ample opportunity for you to find a comfortable approach for each student. Skilled instructors may do this implicitly, but we have found that a quick review serves us well.

8. *Determining assessment strategies.* Assessment strategies may be determined by the programs or may be left to the individual instructor. They could be traditional paper-and-pencil tests, such as the practice GED exams, or they could consist of alternative assessment strategies (see Chapter Seven) such as portfolios. Perhaps the instructors will assess their students based on reflective writing or

on a product emanating from a particular strategy. Whatever the choice, instructors must assure that the assessment strategy stems from the activities undertaken and serves to underscore the objectives identified in the theme unit development process. We encourage a variety of assessment strategies as well as students' input into what assessment practices are meaningful for them.

The sample theme units in Exhibits 5.1 through 5.4 were developed in concrete settings. We urge you to develop your own and to alter these as you go through this process with your learners.

Exhibit 5.1.
Developing a Theme Unit: Becoming a Critical Consumer.

Life experience	Theme
"It seems like my whole paycheck is eaten up at the grocery store. I need to save money or cut back somehow." Marta	Becoming a critical consumer

Forming objectives

1. Using a brainstorming process, ask the learners to think of five things that Marta can do to save money or cut back.
2. Ask the group to suggest what to do about this problem.
3. Using their answers, form objectives.

Sample objectives

A. Learners will identify grocery store sales.
B. Learners will write a family budget.
C. Learners will write a shopping list for one week, reflecting savings.
D. Learners will calculate the costs and savings of food items.
E. Learners will demonstrate understanding of coupons and bulk buying options.
F. Learns will demonstrate understanding of refund policies.
G. Each learner will describe his or her personal shopping style.

Note: Objectives must come from the learners' needs!!

Strategies

1. (A) Have learners find and collect Wednesday ad sections.
2. (A) Ask students to read costs out loud in groups of two.
3. (A) Ask students to compare costs/select best savings.
4. (B) Provide sample budgets and ask students to prepare a budget and identify amount available for food.
5. (B) Invite students to write down everything purchased on last trip to grocery store. Bring receipts to groups of two to analyze purchases.
6. (C) Ask students to write down everything needed for this week.
7. (D) Have students calculate costs and savings with coupons.
8. (E) Invite a guest speaker from Consumer Extension to talk about bulk shopping and storage of food items. Invite a "coupon lady" to class. Ask students to debate pros and cons of using coupons. Have students write a letter to Penny Pincher column with a savings idea.
9. (F) Have students identify criteria for returning items. Give scenarios and have them role-play returning items. Have them write a letter to a company about a defective product.
10. (G) In groups of two, identify and compare shopping styles.

Skills developed

Critical thinking
- Budgeting
- Planning
- Organizing information
- Synthesizing material

Reading
- Reading want ads
- Understanding coupons
- Finding sales

Math
- Basic addition and subtraction
- Percentages

Writing
- Writing a family budget
- Writing a shopping list
- Writing a letter about a defective product

Learning-to-learn
- Practicing active listening skills
- Teamwork
- Giving and receiving feedback
- Awareness of styles and influences on decisions
- Comparing and contrasting information

Formats used

Individual research	Large groups
Individual writing	Dyads
Lecture	Role playing
Think-pair-share	Group discussion
Brainstorming	Small groups

Exhibit 5.2.
Theme Unit: Providing a Safe Environment for Your Children.

Life experience	Theme
"Becoming a parent can be overwhelming. There are so many ways the children can get hurt. Like the stranger hanging over at the school that day. It scares me," said Phyllis. "I know what you mean," said Karen. "I came home and Joey was playing with matches."	Providing a safe environment for your children

Forming objectives

1. Using a think-pair-share approach, ask learners to brainstorm issues of safety for their children.
2. Use a nominal group process to vote on priorities for further exploration.

Sample objectives

A. Learners will understand basic first aid and gain skills in its application: burns, sunburn, choking, cuts, sprains, etc.
B. Learners will identify four safety rules they will teach their children: i.e., playing with matches, crossing the street, turning on burners, hot bath water, etc.
C. Learners will identify ways to tell their children about talking to strangers: answering the door, information on the phone, strangers at school.
D. Learners will identify forms of violence that affect their children: bullies at school, domestic violence, influence of television.

Note: Objectives must come from the learners' needs!!

Strategies

1. (A) Invite a Red Cross instructor to class to demonstrate basic first aid. Have students role-play and practice.
2. (B) Ask learners to brainstorm dangers or safety issues at home: cleaning solvents, matches, neighbor's dog, crossing the street, etc. Identify two responses to each danger. Have them write a script of how to talk to their children and have them practice.
3. (B) Have students use magazines or colored paper to make a safety collage or poster at home with their children.
4. (C) Invite a community liaison police officer to class to talk about safety procedures and how to talk to kids about strangers. Students can ask any questions they want. They should read their pamphlets.
5. (C) Have students write a "magazine" or
   (D) "newletter" on a safety issue. Each one should take one issue. Be sure to include demographic statistics in each article.
6. (C) Encourage students to develop a code safety rule with their children. Practice ways to talk on the telephone and answer questions. Have students write down their feelings about their children's safety.
7. (D) Have learners brainstorm sources of violence in their lives. Use a suggestion circle to identify responses.
8. (D) Invite a Domestic Violence Coalition member to class, listen to sources of violence, and suggest responses.
9. (D) Have groups of two students identify community resources on violence using the phone book.
10. (D) Show excerpts from cartoons, TV shows, rock videos. Ask students to identify the message and respond to the programming with a round-robin writing exercise.

Skills developed

Reading
- Perusing safety pamphlets
- Following diagrams and charts
- Understanding blue pages of the phone book for community resources

Writing
- Script for teaching children
- Newsletter or magazine on safety
- Round-robin response writing
- Journal

Math
- Percentages
- Decimals
- Demographic statistics (3 of 5, 1 of 10)

Learning-to-learn
- Giving and receiving feedback
- Understanding role of authority
- Learning from our people
- Learning with other people
- Working in teams
- Identifying own needs
- Interviewing skills

Critical thinking
- Organizing information
- Synthesizing material
- Making decisions
- Teaching material to another person

Formats used

Lecture	Group brainstorming
Small groups	Round-robin writing
Individual research	Dyads

Exhibit 5.3.

Theme Unit: Practicing Good Nutrition.

Life experience	Theme
"I feel so tired all of the time. I don't have any energy to cook dinner. The kids prefer hot dogs and macaroni and cheese anyway, so it's easier to just use the mixes. That way they don't fuss." Mary Jo	Practicing good nutrition

Forming objectives

1. Using a think-pair-share process, ask the learners to identify five key issues/problems that Mary Jo faces.
2. Ask the group to identify what Mary Jo might do for each problem area. Ask what information she needs.
3. Using the group findings, form objectives.

Sample objectives

A. Learners will demonstrate an understanding of the elements of good nutrition.
B. Learners will identify ways to include their children in a good nutrition plan.
C. Learners will plan nutritious means for a typical week for their family.
D. Learners will identify the benefits of good nutrition and exercise.
E. Learners will identify the elements of a family plan for exercise, healthy snacks, nutritious meals.
F. Learners will demonstrate an understanding of the costs of buying nutritious food.

Note: Objectives must come from the learners' needs‼

Strategies

1. (A) Ask the students to make a poster of the four basic food groups. Supply materials, magazines, paste, scissors, etc. Ask them to make a second poster of their favorite meal and present it to class identifying the elements of the food groups.
2. (A)
    (D) Ask students to brainstorm ways that food affects our behavior and health. Have them develop interview questions and invite a dietician to class to discuss these issues.
3. (B) Have learners keep a daily food journal with their children for a week, writing down everything they eat and drink. Ask them to analyze their eating in light of new learning about food groups. Brainstorm ways to teach their children about healthy eating.
4. (C)
    (E) Have learners prepare a weekly plan for nutritious meals. Ask them to bring a
    (F) favorite recipe to share and one meal idea from their family. Supply various cookbooks. Select nutritious meals. Calculate shopping and budget needs.
5. (D)
    (F) Prepare a simple meal together and discuss barriers to good nutrition and how to overcome them. Take a walk together or do an aerobic activity. Visit the YWCA and discuss the role of exercise in good nutrition with a trainer. Brainstorm ways to exercise every day.
6. (A)
    (F) Invite a representative of the local vegetarian society to discuss food choices. Have learners write a report about the findings. Research the debate about meat eating in the library and the local health food store.

Skills developed

Reading
- Reading cookbooks
- Reading out loud
- Reading forms and applications
- Comprehending ideas

Writing
- Writing meal plans
- Filling out applications
- Summarizing information in paragraph form
- Writing questions
- Writing a report to present to class

Math
- Calculating costs of meals
- Estimating time
- Calculating meal budget
- Multiplying and dividing
- Percentages

Learning-to-learn
- Receiving and giving feedback
- Learning from and with others
- Identifying gaps in knowledge
- Comparing and contrasting information
- Working in teams
- Negotiating
- Using newspaper, library, community agencies as sources of information, apply knowledge to new situation

Formats used

Large-group brainstorming	Small-group debriefing
Individual research	Individual writing
Lecture/guest speaker	Round-robin writing
Field trip	Role playing
Large-group debriefing	

Exhibit 5.4.
Theme Unit: Getting a Good Job.

Life experience	**Theme**
"I got laid off again at the factory. As a temp, we are the first to go. I really need a job that pays enough to feed my family," says Reuben. "I know what you mean," Phyllis responds, "but where are those jobs?"	Getting a good job

Forming objectives

1. Ask the group to identify all of the issues in getting a job. Record their responses: i.e., finding jobs, writing applications, resumes, interviews, training needed, salary, etc.
2. Ask the group to identify three of Reuben's concerns and two ideas that will respond to each concern.

Sample objectives

A. Learners will identify jobs available in the community.
B. Learners will identify skills needed for different careers and training and education options.
C. Learners will identify personal career interests and goals. Learners will establish time lines to achieve goals.
D. Learners will develop job history and personal resumes.
E. Learners will develop interview skills.
F. Learners will become familiar with costs incurred in job transitions (fees, loss of insurance, transportation, etc.).
G. Learners will identify own strengths and challenges in workplace.
H. Learners will become familiar with community job resources.
I. Learners will demonstrate understanding of job descriptions.

Note: Objectives must come from the learners' needs!!

Skills developed

Reading
- Reading the want ads
- Reading class report out loud
- Reading forms and applications

Writing
- Writing resume
- Filling out forms and applications
- Summarizing information in paragraph form
- Writing questions
- Writing a report to present to class

Math
- Calculating costs of resume production
- Estimating time
- Calculating salary needs
- Multiplying and dividing
- Percentages

Learning-to-learn
- Receiving and giving feedback
- Learning from and with others
- Identifying gaps in knowledge
- Comparing and contrasting information
- Teamwork
- Negotiation
- Using library, phone book and community agencies as sources of information

Strategies

1. Have the learners brainstorm their own job interests. In groups of two, have them interview one another using interest and skills inventories to identify each other's skills and strengths.
2. Have students read the want ads in the newspaper each day. Have them bring in the Sunday want ads and identify one community resource for finding jobs. Each student reports on three jobs: the kind of job, skills and education required, salary, application process.
3. Attend a community job fair as a class field trip. Collect information for later reading. Debrief observations.
4. Invite the local job service representative to speak to the class on finding and keeping jobs. Have students prepare interview questions. Ask students to write a paragraph on one key issue.
5. Take students to a career services or placement office. Use the Sigiplus program or other computerized inventory of interests. Ask students to compare the result of this inventory with their group interviews.
6. Ask students to draw the "Shape of their World" identifying influences on their family, career, and job situation. Have each student share their drawing with the group. Use this as a springboard for discussion of personal barriers and strengths or of socioeconomic factors of the job market.
7. Have each student write a list of all of their jobs and volunteer experiences. Ask them to construct a resume and cover letter. Have them trade resumes with another student for critique and feedback. Calculate copying, transportation, and postage costs for application process.
8. Ask students to prepare a family budget to calculate salary needs. Using salary information of various jobs, ask each student to calculate hours of work needed to meet needs.
9. Conduct an interview fair in class. Role-play job interviews with class members, including dress, resume, and cover letters. Invite a personnel manager to class and repeat the process. Debrief.
10. Ask students to provide scenarios of difficult job situations to the class and ask the group to suggest responses. Debrief responses with an employer.

Formats used

Large-group brainstorming	Small-group debriefing
Individual research	Individual writing
Lecture/guest speaker	Round-robin writing
Field trip	Role playing
Large-group debriefing	

Exhibit 5.5.
   Theme Unit (Blank Form).

Life experience	**Theme**

Forming objectives

Sample objectives	**Strategies**

Skills developed

Formats used

CHAPTER 6

Instructional Strategies

In this chapter we discuss several strategies to use with ITB instruction and provide concrete suggestions about using these strategies effectively. While some of these strategies reflect characteristics of effective instruction regardless of the approach used, others flow more naturally from the ways in which instruction is organized in the ITB approach. In many cases, the ideas presented in this chapter derive from the practices of the teachers participating in the integrated project. Whenever possible, we try to identify and acknowledge the source of these strategies.

Building a Good Learning Environment

One of the most important features of the ITB approach is constructing an environment that physically, psychologically, and socially facilitates the overall goals of this form of instruction. But what does it take to have an environment that is conducive to good learning? There are two areas you need to think about: the physical environment and the psychological environment. By attending to some of the suggestions and issues we identify here, you can overcome some of the inhibiting factors to good learning and set the stage for excellent developmental education for adults. We refer you to our earlier discussion on physiological, affective, and cognitive issues for adult learners in Chapters Two and Three.

The Physical Environment

As teachers, we often have to work with what we get. Classroom space is at a premium, and often our classrooms have aspects that may not fit our goals, such as fixed seating, broken chalkboards, and poor ventilation. The teacher's first task, then, is to minimize a room's negative impact on the class session. Recently, when one of the authors arrived in his classroom for that evening's session, the blackboard was filled with writing and no eraser was in sight anywhere. He had to borrow one from an office several doors down the hallway. Fortunately, he had arrived early enough to address this problem before the session started. When one is sharing instructional space, surprises lurk around every corner.

Ideas About a Room that Works

- Keep it uncluttered.
- Make sure each learner has a comfortable place to write.
- If possible, it is helpful for students to have their own file box or mailbox.
- Have all supplies on hand and make sure they are easy to use.
- Make sure the lights are bright and in good working order.
- Be sure the room is as accessible as possible to learners with physical limitations.
- Make sure there is plenty of wall space for flip charts.
- The temperature should be not too hot, not too cold.
- Get the most comfortable, but not sleep-inducing, chairs you can find.
- If you want interaction, make sure people can talk to each other easily. For example, do not have rows of chairs if you expect a discussion to flow.
- If you are going to lecture, make sure everyone will be able to hear. If you use a video, check that everyone can see it from their seats.
- Is the room cheerful? If not, what about displaying flowers or posters or artwork from your learners or their children? Can you have plants to liven up the room?
- Is the room an inviting place for all people? Does it reflect a comfort level for all cultures?
- Is the room free from any one specific religion's symbolism? Is it inclusive of all?

All of this may seem obvious. The idea is to think about it beforehand and build it into your preparation time. Even the best-planned sessions will suffer in an awful room. Ask yourself, "What do *I* need in a room?" Ask your learners what they would like in a room. What does a particular class session need to succeed? Make your own checklist for a good physical environment. Try to obtain what you can, and plan to minimize the effects of what you can't change. (You might even turn this into an object lesson for the learners on institutional constraints and benefits.)

The Psychological Environment

At the psychological level, safety and trust are key to creating a good place to learn. People learn best when they feel safe enough to take some risks, to expose and confront what they do not know. Teachers should take great care in creating a safe, productive environment. We place special emphasis on the need for learners to feel safe or unthreatened when they receive possibly critical feedback. How such feedback is worded and delivered may affect the learning environment profoundly. Picking the right kind of feedback hinges on what the person is ready to hear and what challenges they can face.

There is little risk for the participants when you deliver a content-specific class session. There might not be personal feedback, for example. But longer and more interactive sessions create more exposure for participants. Setting clear ground rules and guidelines and modeling the way you expect people to behave will help create productive learning environments. For example, rules about not making personal attacks or about speaking in turn will facilitate interaction.

Respect for each other is key to creating a safe environment. This includes respect for one's cultural identity, religious heritage, values and beliefs, and personal and physical challenges. Ask your learners how they might demonstrate such respect. Think about how you will demonstrate this respect.

Think through the design of each class session from this perspective. How would you rate the risk? What might be scary for the participants? Are your questions or are the issues you will discuss appropriate? Have you set a positive tone that encourages trust among the learners? Are the goals clear? Is this a class you would feel good about taking? What do your fellow teachers think when you explain your plans to them? Are you prepared to deal with unexpected issues that might arise and to do so in a supportive way?

During our site visits, we gathered ideas that have been particularly effective in creating stimulating and safe classrooms. The *Ideas that Work* materials from the Oregon Adult Basic Education CASAS/GED network is an excellent resource (ABLE Network, n.d.) that we have used and adapted. We urge readers to adapt these to their own environment. The keys to fostering good learning environments are ground rules, skilled use of feedback, clarity about decision making, and stimulating, clear instructional strategies.

Use of Ground Rules

ITB instruction involves learners directly and personally in the learning experience. For this reason, it is usually helpful to use ground rules to guide the work in this kind of environment. Establishing ground rules can help develop a positive and safe psychological climate, making it more conducive to the kind of learning involved in this form of instruction. In this section we discuss what ground rules are and why they should be used, how to establish them, and criteria for selecting ground rules for the particular kinds of groups that will be formed in the instructional process.

What Are Ground Rules and Why Use Them?

Ground rules identify behaviors that help groups function well. A *norm* is a standard, acceptable way of acting regarded as typical for a specific group. A *rule* is a direction for conduct. A *ground rule* is a basic rule of procedure or behavior, such as "No smoking in the classroom," or "Give feedback positively." When norms or ground rules are not stated, discussed, agreed upon, and observed, the members of the group will be inhibited and will participate less openly in order to protect themselves. For example, if a class is exploring the theme of employment and is developing application letters in task groups, an appropriate ground rule might be "Identify another person's strengths, not their deficiencies," or "Assure that each person in the group has shared at least one idea."

In practice, when ground rules are designed to allow open participation and students state differing positions and think independently, an individual participant will usually not believe or act upon the ground rules immediately. After a period of observing and testing the leader, each person will notice if the leader really follows the rules. He or she will also decide whether enough of the other participants accept the rules in order for him or her to feel safe. When the use of the ground rules establishes that disagreement or making a mistake will not bring censure, the individual can spend less energy on self-protection and more on learning. Leaders need to be willing to reinforce the importance of the ground rules by referring to them at the opening of each meeting, by keeping them posted in large and clearly written type so all participants can see them, by calling attention to them as a way of stopping unwanted behaviors, and by reminding people of the protection the ground rules offer.

How Do You Establish Ground Rules in a Group?

Establishing ground rules in an adult learning environment involves several steps:

- Ask the group members to identify elements of classroom environments in which they were comfortable or elements that would make them feel comfortable.

- Negotiate ground rules with the group. If there are safety or administrative rules that are not negotiable, be clear about them. Ask the group to add other rules that are important to them.

- Explain the meaning of each ground rule in one or two sentences.

Choosing Ground Rules for Four Different Types of Groups

The specific ground rules established will depend on the kind of group formed within the instructional process. For our purposes, we can identify four types of learning groups: (1) discovery groups, (2) sharing groups, (3) skill-building or task groups, and (4) planning groups. Some ground rules work well in all four types of groups, but there are instances in which different rules are appropriate. Notice the differences in the four groups. Each of them has a different focus or emphasis.

Discovery Groups.   Discovery groups focus on self-awareness or increasing an awareness of each individual's relationship to a special group, issue, possibility, or problem. The focus of such a group may be on knowledge, values, or both. Learning tasks may include personal values checklists, journal reading, sharing of poems, and lifeboat exercises or other values clarification exercises.

Members need safety and protection to explore and to try out something new. They need to give maximum energy to their individual needs and feelings and minimum energy to performing to meet a standard, pleasing the group, or protecting themselves from censure. These ground rules are appropriate for many types of sharing groups:

1. Everyone participates.
2. Everyone has the right to pass.
3. All opinions and beliefs are honored.
4. Confidentiality is assured.
5. Leader stays in a position of respect for self and others.
6. No side conversations permitted.

The full participation ground rule assumes that everyone, including the leader, will participate at least mentally in each activity. The rule protects the participants from being asked to do something that the leader is not willing to do and asks that everyone attend to what the group is doing.

The right to pass protects each individual, including the leader, from having to speak out, from revealing himself or herself unwillingly. Honoring each person's attitudes, opinions, and beliefs emphasizes that they have helped him or her make sense out of life and therefore have personal validity. This rule also affirms adults' ability to think and to decide for themselves. In addition, it protects the group from the divisiveness of having to decide who is right or wrong when people disagree.

The fourth ground rule of confidentiality (or no gossip) provides protection so that people can role-play new behavior and then decide if they want to keep or discard it. It also encourages people to solve within the group any problems they may have with the group, rather than complaining to outsiders. Take care to check whether the group wants to use this rule, because the leader has no way to enforce it.

The fifth ground rule, that the leader is expected to stay in a position of respect for self and others, protects the participants from criticism and the leader from loss of integrity. The leader is free to express his or her own belief positions, but is not to push it on other people or to apologize for it in order to please the group. This ground rule demands that the leader model respectful, accepting behavior for the group. It does not assume that every behavior is all right, but rather that the needs of each person are important. For example, the leader will not permit one person to dominate the group with constant talking and questions, but will respect that person's need for attention.

The "No side conversations" rule helps the group function as a group and minimizes competition and disruption. In groups composed of experienced group members, this rule may not be needed. It does, however, give the leader an easy way to intervene if members are disturbing the group with whispered conversations or disruptive "aside" comments.

Three of these rules—full participation, the right to pass, and acceptance of everyone's beliefs—are borrowed from the methods used in values clarification. Think about these sample ground rules and consider how you could use each to provide protection so that people can grow.

Sharing and Support Groups.   Sharing and support groups are designed to help members exchange information, feelings, hopes, grief, or concerns. Learning activities might include small-group research on youth gang prevention strategies or sharing stories of adjustment to parenting and brainstorming alternatives to challenges. For the theme of the immigrant experience, members might share stories of their arrival in the United States. Like discovery groups, support groups are places where people need maximum safety. They need to know what is acceptable and what the boundaries are. The same ground rules that are suggested for discovery groups offer protection and set the stage for a collaborative learning atmosphere in sharing groups.

Consistently used, these rules provide protection and permission for people to make their own decisions to grow. They assure a safe place for people to try out new behaviors, change their words, consider their attitudes, and think about their underlying beliefs. The rules provide a framework for self-directed learning. They define people as having worth and protect them from embarrassment if they make mistakes. The ground rules for the discovery groups work well for sharing and support groups. The group may have special considerations they wish to add.

Skill-Building or Task Groups.   Skill-building or task groups are intended to help the members complete specific tasks or increase job, recreational, physical, mental, spiritual, personal, interpersonal, or group skills. Learning tasks might include such things as calculating percentages of markdowns of consumer items, developing word processing skills, or developing oral presentation skills. Skill-building groups focus on developing specific skills of the individuals or the group as a whole (e.g., problem-solving skills). Task groups focus on completing specific assignments or tasks, or addressing problems that they are confronting. Ground rules for skill-building or task groups, for example, will often address safety, use, and care of equipment and guidelines for sharing that equipment.

The "Right to pass" rule is not appropriate here. Since the

purpose of these groups is to learn a set of skills or services, passing doesn't work. Nobody wants a surgeon who decided to pass on learning how to remove an appendix. If you are learning to be a welder, you must learn the safety rules. No passing!

"Confidentiality" is often not appropriate for these groups. While individual members may choose not to gossip about each other's personal concerns, there is no reason to practice confidentiality about the skills or tasks of the group members unless the purpose of the group is such that matters of security, client confidentiality, or competitive edge demand silence.

A basic set of ground rules for skill-building groups could include:

1. Participation in learning concepts, processes, and standards is required of everyone.
2. Listen to all opinions with respect.
3. Separate opinions from facts.
4. Honor time and completion commitments.
5. Observe safety and care for equipment rules.

Task group rules do not differ much from those used in skill-building groups. There may be a difference in the approach to values. People who agree to do a task, especially if it is for pay, are sometimes required to do something that does not fit with their own values. In that case, they have to decide whether to set aside their values and do the task as described, attempt to change the situation, or quit.

The ground rules for a task group might read:

1. Be responsible for your own part of the task.
2. Listen to and consider all suggestions.
3. Meet the standards.
4. Honor time and completion commitments.
5. Observe safety and care of equipment rules.

Often, these rules are understood in the slang of a particular group. One group stated them as:

1. Pull your own weight and help your buddy.
2. No put-downs.
3. Do the job according to the manual.
4. Beat the clock.
5. Follow the OSHA rules, even the stupid ones.

Planning Groups. The members of planning groups meet to plan for the future. They can plan anything from one event for a single individual to the next decade of youth programming for the city. These groups are often referred to as boards, task forces, or committees. Planning-group ground rules will include consequences for commitments not completed on time, methods for evaluating suggestions, and respectful listening to opinions. Ground rules for these groups will vary and will often have similarities to those of the task groups. One group might use "Start and stop on time," while another would use "Start on time and work until the job is finished." One group might say that a majority vote of members present is necessary for making each decision. Another group might use a rule of achieving consensus on major issues if possible or require 75 percent member agreement.

Mixed Groups. As time passes, some groups move from one category to another. Other groups will fall into two or three categories at the same time. This is typical in self-help or growth groups and family literacy programs, where several skills are taught and mutual support is fostered. For example, groups studying a book on esteem and family relationships increase their awareness of their own attitudes and behavior, find out what other parents think, and practice parenting skills at each meeting.

In the case of a group that moves from one type to another, you may need to change the ground rules, or change them for a time. In the example of a parents group, parents who have been using support group rules, but are learning a new skill such as active listening or a new technique such as a suggestion circle, will temporarily use the skill-building rule "Meet the standards."

What to Do When Someone Breaks a Ground Rule

If somebody breaks a ground rule, tell the group that a ground rule has been broken, say which rule was broken, and announce that the group will now deal with that break and make some decisions about this ground rule in the future.[1] Ask people to identify how they felt when the ground rule was broken. Some rules, like confidentiality, are more serious than others and may require more time to discuss. To preserve elements of safety, remind learners to say "I felt" rather than "You made me feel." For example: "This was the first time I have shared in the group. When

---

Note: The ideas we have presented in this section are adapted with permission from Virginia Tardaewether, Even Start Family Literacy, Salem, Oregon.

you told outside of the group, I felt angry." Ask each person to tell what he or she needs now in order to feel safe in the group again. Ask each person, one at a time, if he or she is willing to follow the ground rule of confidentiality in the future.

Renegotiate the ground rules in the way that seems appropriate for your particular group. For example: "We've all agreed to observe the ground rules, so we will continue using them as they are stated." Or: "You have heard that one person does not plan to observe the confidentiality ground rule, so keep that in mind when you choose what to reveal about yourself." Or: "Do we need to add another ground rule to give us further protection and safety?"

You may want to open and close a meeting with an activity to remind people of the ground rules and to check to see how the ground rules are working. Ask several people to share how this meeting would have been different for them if the ground rules had not been stated and posted. Ask about any resentment. Listen to expressions of that resentment without defending or explaining. Ask what people appreciate. Thank everyone for participating.

Feedback

Feedback is a very important instructional strategy to facilitate adult learning. Feedback is a key ingredient in a safe and high-quality learning environment. Facilitators require skill in giving feedback to their learners.

Tips on Giving Feedback

Some ways of providing feedback are more effective than others. As an instructor, you will need to keep in mind the characteristics of effective and ineffective feedback. You will also want to help your learners learn how to receive feedback as well. In this section, we provide some tips on how to provide feedback as well as help your learners develop skill in receiving it.

Here are some tips on giving feedback effectively:

Feedback Is Effective When It Is:	**Feedback Is Not Effective When It Is:**
Specific	General
Descriptive	Judgmental
Timely	An untimely rehashing of all past errors
About something that can be changed	About an unchangeable attribute

Feedback Is Effective When It Is:	**Feedback Is Not Effective When It Is:**
For good of receiver	For good of (relief of) giver
Stated with care and concern	Stated angrily or in an attacking fashion

Tips on Receiving Feedback

It is often not easy to hear feedback, whether it is minor criticisms or suggestions for drastic change. Receiving feedback places one in a vulnerable position. Many people have not learned how to receive constructive feedback. Plus, some learners may not have had good experiences with feedback in past schooling situations. For many, receiving feedback may have felt like a massive put-down, causing a devastating loss of self-esteem, more than a positive suggestion for improvement that resulted in a sense of assurance as study continued.

Learners and teachers alike benefit from evaluation and can best hear the feedback and input by remembering these pointers:

- Be quiet.
- Don't defend.
- Realize that some necessary behavior will get negative feedback. We all make mistakes from time to time. It is important, for example, not to make mistakes in the future that can jeopardize the safety or health of fellow workers.
- Avoid speculation.
- If you don't understand, ask for clarification.
- One person's opinion is just that; you may want to check it out.
- Information is part of formative evaluation; ask "How can I do it better next time?"

Suggestion Circles

One of the teachers in our project uses the suggestion circle as a tool for collecting ideas from learners and fostering mutual support among learners. It is a problem-solving tool that offers high-quality alternatives and is a powerful way to share information and ideas quickly. The suggestion circle provides a way to honor someone with a problem and meet the needs of individuals in the group without tying up the group for extended periods of time.

This technique treats everyone in the group as potential "experts" who have knowledge to share with the learner who has a problem. The suggestion circle and brainstorming are both techniques for collecting ideas. While brainstorming (discussed later) stimulates creativity, the suggestion circle brings out the wisdom of the group. When the person asking for help seems to be seeking information about alternative solutions to a specific problem, use the suggestion circle to activate clear thinking.

For example, Joan may come to the group with a complaint that her neighbor does not pick up her children on time, making Joan late to their adult education class. Her tardiness may disrupt the class's work. The facilitator could take the following steps:

1. Contract with Joan to be a listener, to accept each suggestion with no comment other than a "Thank you."

2. Ask her to state one problem in a clear, concise way.

3. Ask someone else to make a written list of the suggestions so that Joan can give full attention to listening.

4. Ask the people in the suggestion circle to center their bodies, think carefully for a moment about possible solutions to the problem, and give one high-quality, one- or two-sentence "You could . . ." or "I would . . ." suggestion. They are not to comment on or evaluate each other's suggestions.

5. When the suggestions have been given, remind Joan to take the suggestions home and decide which to use.

A suggestion circle of twelve people takes from three to five minutes to complete. While this might seem like quite a short time, it is doable. Remember, the goal is to give the learner concise and clear suggestions, not to exhaust all possible solutions or to engage in a protracted discussion. While other group members may share the problem, individual problems can also derail the instructional goals for a given session. The suggestion circle meets the need of the person with the problem, involves other learners, and allows the teacher to return to the class activities.

Suggestion Circles or Discussions?

Teachers may ask themselves, "How do I know when to lead a suggestion circle and when to have a discussion?" Each has specific advantages. A discussion provides time for social interaction, for getting to know people, for expressing feelings and concerns, for offering empathy, and for developing intimacy.

The disadvantages of discussions are that they take an indeterminate amount of time and they sometimes become competitive rather than helpful. People may play win-lose as in, "If you dislike my idea, I am no good (or you are no good)." They sometimes make comparisons as in, "Her suggestion is better than his." They may play right-wrong as in, "It isn't fair for you to consider our ideas equally—mine is right and his is wrong." Sometimes they play king of the hill as in, "My idea is the only one that counts." All of these competitive interactions tend to draw attention from the ideas to the people and to block the free flow of thoughts. Learners may wander off course.

The quality of contributions to either a discussion or a suggestion circle depends on the level of competence of the people in the group. During a discussion, the person with the most helpful ideas may not share them, because people contribute to a discussion according to their habits of speaking and sharing, not according to their level of expertise. A suggestion circle has the advantage of efficiency. It exposes people to a maximum of options in a limited period of time. It is also an effective way of gathering information from each person present. It is not advantageous to use the suggestion circle if people want leisurely social time more than they want ideas or options.

Why Use a Suggestion Circle?

What are the benefits to the individual who asks for a circle? Is the circle of value to the other people in the group? What are the benefits for the group? How does leading a suggestion circle benefit the leader?

Individual. There are many rewards for the individual seeking options. The person with the problem can receive: (1) the benefit of the experiences of a whole group of people; (2) help in clarifying a fuzzy problem; (3) the support that comes from having a group of people take his or her problem seriously; (4) reassurance that there is more than one possible solution to his or her problem; (5) encouragement to take responsibility for resolving the problem; and (6) repeated invitations to think clearly.

Others. Everyone participating in the circle has the chance to practice evaluative thinking, attentive listening, and clear and uncluttered communication skills. In addition, they have the opportunity to listen carefully to and respect the values and experiences of each person present.

Group. The group's efficiency is strengthened by the fact that it has a quick way to address a wide variety of problems. Repeated comparisons between open discussions and suggestion circles in the same group reveal that a three- to five-minute suggestion circle usually yields more options than a twenty-minute general discussion. The group's effectiveness is increased by its ability to tap all of the members' resources in an efficient way. The suggestion circle's structure honors all individuals, which enhances the group's general health and well-being.

Leader.   The benefits to the leader include: (1) the opportunity to offer help without the expectation that he or she will be an authority; (2) protection from the temptation to talk at length on a subject about which other members may also have information; (3) protection from the flattery of a group that expects the leader to have all the answers and the hazards of their anger when she doesn't; and (4) a way for her to rechannel group members who play disruptive games.

Why Is the Suggestion Circle Such a Powerful Tool?

People who use circles notice many aspects of the tool's power. A suggestion circle includes everyone, honors everyone, does not degrade anyone's ideas, encourages clear, concise thinking and speaking, and is efficient.

A less obvious aspect of the circle's power is that it expects the listener to think more. Not only does the person become responsible for evaluating, choosing, and rejecting ideas, but must also negotiate the circle's conflicting "good advice." For example, the individual may have asked, "What should I do about my teenage daughter's room? It is a mess most of the time." One response might be, "Review the housekeeping rules with her, set consequences, and carry through." Another suggestion may be, "Close the door." F. Scott Fitzgerald once said, "The test of a first-rate intelligence is the ability to hold two opposing ideas in mind at the same time and still retain the ability to function." Considering conflicting responses often helps the person move from a stuck, helpless position to one of decision and action.

What If People Don't Want to Use Suggestion Circles?

There are three main reasons people in your group may not want to use suggestion circles. The first and most obvious is that they may not, in fact, want to solve the problem; they may just want to spend some time talking about it. Many people enjoy passing time with the social discourse of "Ain't it awful" or "My problem is worse than your problem." The learners may play out this resistance with some of the following comments:

> Yes, but. . . . Your ideas won't help me.

> Poor me. . . . Listen while I tell you at great length how awful things are for me.

> What if. . . . As long as I tell you what could happen, I won't have to accept responsibility for solving my problem.

> If it weren't for him. . . . I am not responsible. If only the other person would change, the problem would be solved.

> Ain't it awful. . . . Let's talk about how bad the whole world is so I can avoid my responsibility in solving this problem.

> Mine's bigger. . . . I don't want to help you solve your problem; I want you to listen to how much worse things are for me than they are for you.

If this is the case in your group, structure some social time before you bring the group focus to problem solving.

A second reason a person may resist a suggestion circle is that he may be convinced there is no solution to his problem or that only one or two possible solutions are acceptable. This is called "either-or" thinking and is very common. If we use this type of thinking, we might benefit from the suggestion circle, but we might also resist it. At a later time, when we are more receptive to hearing alternatives, we will welcome the many options that a circle provides.

The third reason people don't want to use a suggestion circle is that they have not yet experienced the power of the circle or have been subjected to poorly led circles. By using the leadership checklist in Exhibit 6.1, you can assess the quality of the suggestion circles you lead.[2]

Dealing with Barriers to Suggestion Circles

People sometimes throw up barriers to the success of the learning endeavor, whether it is a suggestion circle, another group task, or a review exercise. They often do so unintentionally. To strengthen your ability to lead a crisp, helpful suggestion circle or any other instructional task, we recommend that you practice handling barriers in a supportive situation. Practice on your own family or collect a group of friends or colleagues to help you!

---

[2] From the *I*CANS* Project, Washington State Board for Community & Technical Colleges. Originally provided by Deane Gradous. Reprinted with permission.

Exhibit 6.1.

Checklist for Leading a Suggestion Circle Clearly.

_____ I explained clearly to the people in the group how a suggestion circle works.

_____ I posted the suggestion circle poster.

_____ I helped the focus person clarify his or her situation so that I, the focus person (the member seeking a solution), and the group had a common understanding of the problem.

_____ I made a contract with the focus person to listen to all the suggestions offered and to say only "Thank you," and I supported the focus person in keeping that contract.

_____ I made clear that the "Thank you" was for the person's willingness to give a suggestion and was not a comment on the quality of the suggestion.

_____ I reminded the group to offer their best ideas one at a time in a concise sentence or two, and I praised them for doing that.

_____ I reminded myself and the group of the ground rules, particularly the right to pass, and enforced them as needed.

_____ I offered the opportunity to have someone in the group write down the suggestions for the focus person.

_____ I returned to group members who passed the first time around in case they wished to offer a suggestion later.

_____ I invited the focus person to consider the suggestions and to use them in a way that fit for him or her. I invited the focus person to do something about the situation and report back to the group, but exerted no pressure to do so.

_____ I ran the suggestion circle in three to ten minutes, depending on the size of the group.

_____ If there were more than twenty people, I divided them into groups of ten to fifteen and got others to help so that we could run simultaneous circles.

Here is a list of barriers that participants in suggestion circles sometimes use.[3] They:

Ramble.

Say, "There is no solution anyway."

Distract from discussion or change the topic.

Go on and on about their own problems.

Play "Ain't it awful" or dwell on difficulty.

Say, "Mary's idea is best," or add judgments.

---

[3] The list of barriers was collected at the Yakima and Seattle Suggestion Circle Book Editor's Meeting at Packwood, Washington, March 1984. Used with permission from the I*CANS Project, ABLE Network of Washington.

Comment, "Your answer was really good."

Comment, "I didn't like any of those answers."

Say, "I tried that."

Ask for more information after the circle starts. (This could be a defensive move to derail the work of the group, delay or postpone it, etc.)

Speak out of turn.

Interrupt.

Disrupt.

Offer more than one suggestion.

Play, "I have another suggestion and another and another."

Don't pay attention—read a book.

Talk to neighbors.

Attend to someone else.

Get in a power struggle with the leader.

Make a value judgment on the importance of the problem.

When barriers appear, you can:

- Write each barrier on a separate slip of paper. Or you may want to use the barriers listed above, or others.
- Give each person a slip and ask people to role-play the barrier written on their slip.
- Lead a discussion on the meaning of the barrier to the individual or the group.
- After the discussion, ask people to say what you did that worked well.

Record that information. Celebrate your skill. Ask people to comment on what you could have done to strengthen your leadership. Write those suggestions down and think about which ones you will use. Practicing this exercise not only increases the leader's skills, but also strengthens each group member's ability to confront barriers in an effective way.

When a group participant rambles, restate the question and say, "Is that what you meant?" or ask the person to choose one specific part of the problem for this discussion. For example, Claire may say, "I want a new career. I've tried lots of things and I've gone to college and I'm buried in credits, but I don't know what I want." You could say, "Claire, would you like people to suggest resources you could use to help you choose a new career?"

If the person offering the suggestion uses more than two

sentences, interrupt immediately and say, "Please give your answer in one or two sentences." If a person says, "I agree with Vicki," interrupt and say, "Please give your suggestion even if it is similar to one we already heard." Or you could ask people to write their suggestions on a card and then read it and hand it to the focus person. This may intimidate poor writers and poor spellers, but also offers a chance to practice writing. (This is not the time to correct spelling, however.)

You can deal with most barriers by saying, "Remember the rules of the suggestion circle," and then repeating the rule that applies. The leader can walk around the circle and face each person in an attentive, respectful way, saying, "Do you have a suggestion?"

What if, after the circle is complete, someone says, "You can try all those ideas on your kid if you want, but they won't work. We've tried them all!" You can say, "Different things work in different families. Vicki will decide what she wants to do." You might add, "Would you like a circle? People in this group have lots of ideas."

Brainstorming

Brainstorming is a method for generating a list of thoughts, ideas, and views about a given topic. It is a quick way to help spark new and innovative ideas from a group and invites a large number of options while stimulating the group's creativity. It does not generate in-depth analysis or answers and does not allow a critique of each idea.

This technique can be used in a wide variety of circumstances with almost any size and type of group covering almost any subject. It is highly participatory and can be used as an icebreaker to help everyone feel a part of the group. It is appropriate whenever you want to generate as many ideas as possible on a subject. It is not to be used when you already know the answers you want and wish for the participants to "guess" them correctly.

A brainstorming session takes from five minutes to several hours to complete. Allow more time for larger groups or, if you have another facilitator, break a larger group into two and compare results! One facilitator can also call on people, while the other writes down the ideas to expedite the process.

Depending on your goal, you can add steps to the brainstorming process. For example, if you have brainstormed participants' expectations of a workshop, you could review the list and discuss what will be addressed and what will not. If you brainstorm ideas for future work, you may want to add a step to synthesize and consolidate the list. With the group's approval, you may also add other items to the list that the group didn't mention. You can use the basic brainstorming technique in combination with many other methods.

Brainstorming is especially useful in giving the participants a stake in the session; it creates ownership over and commitment to the process. Be sure that you explain the rules. It is best to post the rules so that the participants can see them. Brainstorming is a valuable technique in having everyone participate and work from somewhat of an equal footing. Be sure to have flip charts and markers ready and assure that all participants can see the recording of the suggestions.

The procedure is as follows:

1. Ask the person to state one problem in a clear, concise way.
2. Ask the person to close their eyes and imagine they are in a time and place where this problem is solved, then to open their eyes and think about possible solutions to the problem.
3. Ask each person to write down five or six possible solutions.
4. On the chalkboard or flip chart paper, write the first suggestion from one person's list. Ask everyone in the room to brainstorm off that idea—to give every idea they think of without evaluating its possibility or practicality.
5. Repeat the first idea from each person's list and as many more as the focus person wants or as the group wishes to take time for. Be sure to include all people at least once!
6. You may want to give the lists to someone assigned as a "recorder" for summary or evaluation. That person will report back to the group. This must be done carefully so that the group does not feel "corrected" or lose ownership in the process. If the recorder wants help with the summary or evaluation and the group agrees to help: (1) ask the recorder to set guidelines and ask the group to use these guidelines when evaluating each idea, or (2) group ideas into categories and select the two or three most valuable ideas from each category. These ideas then become the bases for the group's action or plan.

Key Rules for Brainstorming

- Everyone speaks.
- Don't evaluate ideas. Even the ones that seem off the wall go on the flip chart!
- Don't have discussions about ideas during brainstorming.
- Record participants' words exactly! Don't reinterpret.
- Phrase ideas concisely.

- Don't make any speeches.
- Generate lots and lots of ideas.
- Be creative and outrageous.
- Combine or elaborate others' ideas.
- Have fun!

Brainstorming for Introverts

You can use a much more controlled process or style of "brainstorming" when the ideas are harder to come up with or the group is fairly quiet:

- Clarify the question that everyone should answer.
- Ask everyone to write down as many answers as they can think of without talking it over.
- Go around the group and get one answer from everyone, then go back around until you have exhausted the possibilities.
- For repeat answers, put a check next to the statement on the chart.

Consensus Decision Making

In consensus decision making, group members work together rather than competing against each other. The goal is to reach a decision to which all group members consent. This doesn't mean that the group must completely agree, but that all members agree that they can live with the decision.

There are key assumptions about consensus decision making. Because the decision must be acceptable to many people, must meet a variety of standards, and involves the expertise of all participating, consensus decision making tends to produce high-quality decisions. A decision that will meet all the members' needs requires a wide array of proposals, ideas, and creative thinking. The involvement required of group members in the process of making the decision results in a high level of commitment to the decision. Consensus decision making requires that members value others' opinions, the group, and cooperation.

It is easy to understand consensus in contrast with other styles of decision making, such as majority rule or autocratic modes. We can conceive of types of decision making as being on a continuum. The list below reflects this progression. Group members participate the least under the autocratic style, while they have the highest degree of involvement in consensus decision making.

Style of Decision Making Characteristics

Autocratic	All group members rely on the resources and decision making of one person
Autocratic with polling	One person makes the decision after asking what other group members think
Minority rule	A committee representing the group makes the decision
Majority rule	Each group member has an equal vote and the opinion of the majority is selected
Consensus	Group members work together to develop a decision to which all may consent

There are important differences between majority rule and consensus, although they are at the same end of the continuum.

Majority Rule	**Consensus**
Win-lose approach, divisive arguing of "sides"	Group development and ownership of ideas
Opinions of unequal influence, depending on speaker	Emphasis on cooperation and compromise, not persuasion about particular points
Choices for voting reduced to two	Wide range of decisions and ideas presented and critiqued
Possible emergence of distinct minority, sabotaging decision	Group ownership of final outcome

Teachers should select the style of decision making they would like their learners to understand and use.

Assessment of a Group's Readiness for Consensus Decision Making

The following may serve as guidelines or prerequisites when you assess a group's readiness to begin consensus decision making.

1. *Unity of purpose.* The members have a common purpose or base that has brought them to the group.

2. *Equal access to power.* Each member of the group feels that she or he has an equal role in the group.

3. *Autonomy from external structures.* The group must have the

freedom to make and implement its decisions without interference or disruption from an external authority.

4. *Time and patience.* The process of consensus decision making cannot be rushed. The group must be willing to spend time and energy tending to relationships among members.

5. *Practice.* The group must be willing to develop and practice the skills of consensus decision making.

The Role of Members' Attitudes in Consensus Decision Making

Group members' attitudes are critical to the successful use of consensus as a decision-making process in the instructional setting. While some attitudes are conducive to consensus, others make its use more difficult to implement. We can characterize these kinds of attitudes in the following way:

Attitudes Impeding Consensus	**Attitudes Supporting Consensus**
Competition	Cooperation
Lack of interest in others	Mutual trust among members
Desire to control group or its work	Common ownership of ideas
Suppression of feelings and conflict	Attention given to feelings and conflict
Reliance on authority	Equalization of power

Shape of the World—An Exercise in Observation

This is a very stimulating exercise that helps a group share their perceptions of the most important things happening in the world.[4] It develops members' interest in the forces changing the world for better or for worse. If group members come from very different backgrounds, sharing the variety of perceptions can stretch people's insights. It may be advisable to do a listening exercise before starting, to ensure that people try to understand each other's point of view. If the exercise is done in this spirit, it can create a basis of trust in a very diverse group and provide a common experience for many types of analysis.

---

[4] Reprinted with permission from the Center of Concern. Material originally from Anne Hope and Sally Timmel, *Training for Transformation: A Handbook for Community Workers* (Vols. 1–3) (Gweru, Zimbabwe: Mambo Press, 1984).

Procedure

Ask the participants to form mixed groups of five and to sit around tables where flip chart paper, markers, crayons, tape, and individual papers are provided. Explain that there are five steps in the exercise. Describe each step, illustrating each one on flip chart paper on the wall. The exercise should take about 2½ to 3 hours.

1. Main Illustration
   a. Ask each person to draw a circle on a plain piece of paper. Explain that this circle represents the world in which the participants live.
   b. Ask, "If you could draw a picture (or a symbol) of the world, what would be its main illustration (its main theme)?" Give time for each person to make their own drawing on a separate sheet of paper.
   c. Ask each person to share in their small group what they were trying to express in their drawing.
   d. Then ask each group to make a common picture on flip chart paper that includes everyone's idea. They should either plan together a new drawing that includes all the ideas, or they should draw different ideas in different parts of the circle. (Warn them not to draw the circle too large or to draw outside the circle, because they will have to use the outer space for arrows later.)

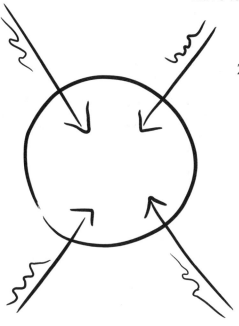

2. Future New Impacts
   a. Ask each small group, "What do you believe is having an impact on the world now, and over the next few years, what will continue to affect it strongly?" Have them discuss this.
   b. Have them reflect their answers by drawing and labeling arrows going into the circle. Arrows going directly into the center show the most direct impact, while arrows that do not go into the center describe a less direct impact.

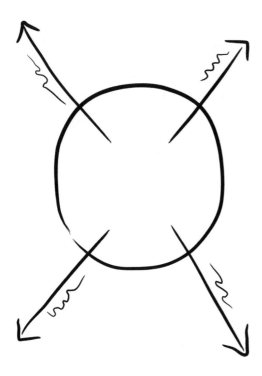

3. Influences Dying Out in the Future
   a. When the small groups have finished the above task, ask them, "What things are dying out in the world now or will continue to do so in the next few years?" Have them discuss this.
   b. They should reflect their answers graphically by drawing and labeling arrows going out of the circle. Arrows leaving from the center represent important influences that are dying out, while arrows leaving from less central parts of the circle describe weaker influences that are fading away.

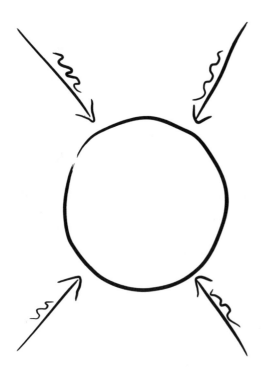

4. Long-Range Impact
   a. When the small groups have finished the above task, ask them, "What things do you believe will one day have an impact on the world, but are now five, ten, or more years away?"
   b. Have them reflect their ideas by drawing and labeling arrows leading up to but not penetrating the circle.

5. Implications
   a. When the group members have completed the above tasks, ask each person to answer in writing, "What is the major insight this process has given me about these issues and our group process?" (Or, what does this mean to me and our group?)
   b. After about five minutes of quiet time, ask the small groups to discuss their points and then to write on flip chart paper a summary of the insights and implications they have discussed.
   c. Share these implications in the whole group. This can be a very useful basis for further work in the group. Each group is asked to post their summary, and everyone can then walk around looking at each one and asking questions.

Overview of Selected Cooperative Learning Structures

There are numerous kinds of cooperative learning strategies that you can use with ITB instruction. We have listed some helpful resources in the References at the end of this book. Exhibit 6.2, adapted from Spencer Kagan (1989), summarizes many of these strategies.

Exhibit 6.2.
Overview of Selected Cooperative Learning Structures.

Structure	Brief description	Academic/social functions
Team building		
Round-robin	Each student in turn shares something with his or her teammates	Expressing ideas and opinions, creation of stories. Equal participation, getting acquainted with teammates.
Class building		
Corners	Each student moves to a corner of the room that represents a teacher-determined alternative. Students discuss within corners, then listen to and paraphrase ideas from other corners.	Seeing alternative hypotheses, values, problem-solving approaches. Knowing and respecting different points of view, meeting classmates.
Communication building		
Match nine	Students attempt to match the arrangement of objects on another student's grid using oral communication only.	Vocabulary development. Communication skills, role-taking ability.
Mastery		
Numbered heads together	The teacher asks a question, students consult to make sure everyone knows the answer, then one student is called upon to answer.	Review, checking for knowledge, comprehension. Tutoring.
Color-coded co-op cards	Students memorize facts using a flash card game. The game is structured so that there is a maximum probability of success at each step, moving form short-term to long-term memory. Scoring is based on improvement.	Memorizing facts. Helping. Praising.
Pairs check	Students work in pairs within groups of four. Within pairs students alternate—one solves a problem while the other coaches. After every two problems, the pair checks to see if they have the same answers as the other pair.	Practicing skills. Helping, praising.
Concept development		
Three-step interview	Students interview each other in pairs, first one way, then the other. Students each share with the group information they learned in the interview.	Sharing personal information such as hypotheses, reactions to a poem, conclusions from a unit. Participation, listening.
Think-pair-share	Students think to themselves about a topic provided by the teacher; they pair up with another student to discuss it; they then share their thoughts with the class.	Generating and revising hypotheses, inductive reasoning, application. Participation, involvement.
Team word webbing	Students write simultaneously on a piece of chart paper, drawing main concepts, supporting elements, and bridges representing the relation of ideas in a concept.	Analysis of concepts into components, understanding multiple relations among ideas, differentiating concepts. Role taking.

Structure	Brief description	Academic/social functions
	Multifunctional	
Round table	Each student in turn writes one answer as a paper and pencil are passed around the group. With simultaneous round table more than one pencil and paper is used at once.	Assessing prior knowledge, practicing skills, recalling information, creating cooperative art. Team building, participation.
Inside-outside circle	Students stand in pairs win two concentric circles. The inside circle faces out; the outside circle faces in. Students use flash cards or respond to teacher questions as they rotate to each new partner.	Checking for understanding, review, processing, helping. Tutoring, sharing, meeting classmates.
Partners	Students work in pairs to create or master content. They consult with partners from other teams. They then share their products or understanding with the other partner pair in their team.	Mastery and presentation of new material, concept development. Presentation and communication skills.
Jigsaw	Each student on the team becomes an "expert" on one topic by working with members from other teams assigned the corresponding topic. Upon returning to their teams, each one in turn teaches the group, and students are all assessed on all aspects of the topic.	Acquisition and presentation of new material, review, informed debate. Interdependence, status equalization.
Co-op	Students work in groups to produce a particular group product to share with the whole class; each student makes a particular contribution to the group.	Learning and sharing complex material, often with multiple sources, evaluation, application, analysis, synthesis. Conflict resolution, presentation skills.

Source: Kagen, S. "The Structural Approach to Cooperative Learning." *Educational Leadership.* 47, 4: 12–15. Reprinted by permission of the Association for Supervision and Curriculum Development. Copyright © 1989 ASCD. All rights reserved.

CHAPTER 7

Assessing ITB Instruction

Our thinking about the role of assessment in ITB instruction is grounded in the work of "authentic assessment" (Schneider & Clarke, 1995). The overall goal of assessment, from the perspective of ITB instruction, is to help achieve the learners' educational objectives. Assessment provides feedback on the extent of that learning and the effectiveness of various aspects of the program in contributing to the learners' progress. While there are other reasons for assessing instruction, which we will also discuss here, we believe these efforts should be in the service of this broad goal.

In this sense, assessment is more than testing for student gains in academic skills, using standardized instruments or tests. While gains in academic skill may be one focus of assessment, it is actually a powerful process for documenting student growth along several dimensions, as well as for gauging the effectiveness of instructional practices (Angelo & Cross, 1993). Assessment is also used to communicate the program's effectiveness to the community and to outside agencies.

Thus, assessment involves an assortment of means for collecting a variety of information. Furthermore, in planning and implementing ITB instruction, educators use assessment continuously to guide their work with adult learners. They use assessment early on to determine what students should learn. Educators continue to use assessment to select the theme, make decisions about instructional methods and materials, identify student gains in knowledge and skills, and communicate the merit and worth of the program to others.

Several groups are interested in the information generated through assessment. Learners want to know the extent to which they are making progress toward their goals and how their performance matches others' expectations. Teachers are interested in seeing how effective their instruction is and how appropriate the curriculum is for their students. Funding agencies want to be sure that their financial support is not wasted by ensuring that the program is effective and that it compares favorably to other programs. Finally, the community has an investment in the program in terms of its ability to prepare individuals for the world of work and to help them become productive family members and citizens. So, it is important to approach the topic of assessment seriously and in a comprehensive manner.

Figure 7.1 depicts all the different areas that could be included in an assessment process (Adult Basic Literacy Educators Network, n.d.). Among the pieces of assessment illustrated in this diagram are factors that focus on:

- The learner (e.g., diagnostic assessment, monitoring progress, competencies, learner goals, learner outcomes)
- The program or curriculum (e.g., program goals, standards, accountability, costs)
- The teacher or the instructional process (e.g., teacher training, performance assessment)

Not all educators will want to use all these factors in their assessment. The metaphor of the puzzle is appropriate to the process of deciding upon and implementing a form of assessment. The staff of each program usually makes a programwide decision on which factors are most important to the program and which can reasonably be addressed effectively, given the resources available.

Assessment of Learners

Standardized tests have traditionally been used as a means of evaluating student progress. In many developmental education programs for adults, they continue to be the primary means by which teachers demonstrate learner progress and program effectiveness. These tests, however, focus only on academic skills and provide a limited picture of the student's ability. Other skills emphasized by the ITB approach and stressed by others (Carnevale, Gainer, & Meltzer, 1988) as important in today's society, such as analysis, critical thinking, problem solving, creativity, and application and performance (Angelo & Cross, 1993), are virtually ignored by most current standardized tests used in these programs. Thus, the

Figure 7.1.
Assessment Systems: Putting the Pieces Together.

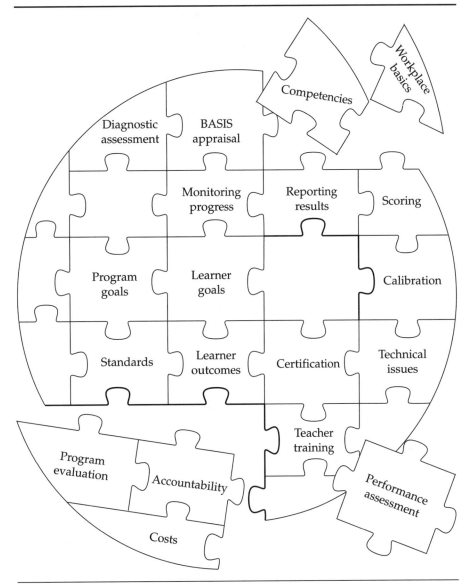

Reprinted with permission from the *I*CANS* Project, Washington State Board for Community & Technical Colleges.

teacher's approach to assessment within an ITB approach needs to be multidimensional, including standardized tests, observed behaviors, products or work samples, student self-report, or other methods that the instructor selects.

Steps to Help Develop a Learner Assessment Process

When approaching learner assessment in this comprehensive and holistic manner, it is helpful to think of the process in terms of a number of important steps. We have listed and briefly described these steps below:

- Assessment should include reading, writing, math, and other academic competencies that the program intends to develop in its learners.

- Teachers and learners should also select process skills to be included in the assessment (e.g., problem solving, critical thinking, interpersonal skills).

- The teacher should select and use methods of assessment for each of the targeted skills areas. Methods of assessment can include formal or standardized tests, observed behaviors, self-report, student products (such as writing), or other procedures that the instructor considers useful.

- The educator should record in his or her instructional plan whatever skills the learners need to work on. The ITB approach works most effectively if the educator identifies some goals that the learners share.

- The teacher should use the results of student performance on these assessment procedures to plan instruction for individuals and for the group as a whole.

- Interim and postassessment procedures should be used to ascertain student progress and the effectiveness of the instructional processes being used. These procedures should also include student products and can be placed in student portfolios.

An Example of an Alternative Assessment Process

Portfolio assessment is a promising alternative to the use of standardized tests to measure learner progress and growth. It effectively addresses the multidimensional ways in which learning occurs in an integrated approach to instruction. According to the Northwest Regional Laboratory, a student portfolio is

> a purposeful collection of student work that tells the story of the student's efforts, progress, or achievement in (a) given area(s). This collection must include student participation in selection of portfolio content; the guidance for selection; the criteria for judging merit; and evidence of student reflection (Adult Basic Literacy Educators Network, n.d., pp. 2–73).

Comprehensive treatment of the topic of portfolio assessment is beyond the scope of this chapter and the intention of this *Guide*. We will, however, briefly discuss a few important characteristics of portfolio assessment.

When portfolios are used as a form of assessment, the purpose of the portfolio needs to be clearly defined. A portfolio is not just a random or ad hoc collection of student work, but is designed with specific purposes in mind. These purposes can range from an application for admission to postsecondary education study to evidence of specific workplace skills to a simple demonstration of accomplishments.

The teacher should develop guidelines to help determine what should go in the portfolio. Although the level of structure that these guidelines provide may vary from program to program, it is generally advisable to give at least general categories from which learners can choose items to represent their work.

Given the overall goal of assessment as fostering learner growth, the students themselves should select specific pieces of work to go into the portfolio. This characteristic increases the likelihood that the assessment process itself is educative, involving the learners' skills in critical thinking, problem solving, and decision making.

Whatever selection process is used, the portfolio should reflect a rich array of student knowledge and skill, be grounded in realistic contexts, provide a profile to students and others of what is valued, mirror the processes used to accomplish the work, and be an integral part of the instructional process. Typical portfolios might reflect the criteria used for selecting and judging the work, as well as samples of the learners' work at various points in their study. Samples might include student essays, videotaped sessions demonstrating interviewing or other interpersonal skills, budgets prepared for a learner's context and for a particular period of time, descriptions and evaluations of student performances that peers or teachers completed, and the learners' written thoughts on their own progress toward their educational goals. In considering these various sources, educators and learners should keep in mind that portfolio assessment needs to be continual.

Numerous resources that focus on portfolio assessment are available to educators of adults interested in alternative assessment processes. We have listed a few here, and others are located in the Resources at the end of this *Guide*.

Arter, J. (1990). *Using portfolios in instruction and assessment.* Portland, OR: Northwest Regional Educational Laboratory. (ERIC Document Reproduction Service No. ED 328 586)

Focuses on helping learners engage in self-reflection and self-assessment.

Auerbach, E. R. (1992). *Making meaning, making change: Participatory curriculum development for adult ESL literacy.* Washington, DC: Center for Applied Linguistics.

Represents a process of conceptualizing assessment within instruction in an ESL family literacy context.

Fingeret, H. (n.d.). *It belongs to me: A guide to portfolio assessment in adult education programs.* (ERIC Document Reproduction Service No. ED 359 352)

Gomez, M. L., Graue, M. E., & Bloch, M. N. (1991). Reassessing portfolio assessment: Rhetoric and reality. *Language Arts, 68,* 620–628.

Examines how using portfolio assessment can change a teacher's work.

Graves, D. H., & Sunstein, B. S. (Eds.). (1992). *Portfolio portraits.* Portsmouth, NH: Heinemann.

Teachers describe their experiences with using portfolio assessment. Contains information on helping learners assess their own work and using portfolios for larger assessment processes.

Lytle, S. L., Belzer, A., Schulz, K., & Vannozzi, M. (1989). Learner-centered literacy assessment: An evolving process. In A. Fingeret & P. Jurmo (Eds.), *Participatory literacy education* (pp. 53–64). San Francisco: Jossey-Bass.

Description of one adult literacy program's effort to implement an alternative assessment process.

Paulson, F. L., Paulson, P. R., & Meyer, C. A. (1991). What makes a portfolio a portfolio. *Educational Leadership, 48*(2), 60–63.

Presents guidelines for using portfolios.

Tierney, R. J., Carter, M. A., & Desai, L. E. (1991). *Portfolio assessment in the reading-writing classroom.* Norwood, MA: Christopher-Gordon.

Presents a fair amount of information on the theory and practice of portfolio assessment, including the overarching philosophy that guides this approach, and step-by-step descriptions of the process.

Fostering Self-Assessment Skills Among Learners

Learners, especially those who have had unsuccessful schooling experiences, may find themselves uncertain about whether they have mastered the material at hand. Past assessment experiences may have been simply "top-down"—an authority figure gave the final word on the level of mastery. Our goal is to have the learners become aware of their own mastery of the theme and gain confidence in that mastery. You can encourage the learners to ask themselves the following questions as they determine their progress in learning:

- Am I using a variety of effective methods to solve problems?

- Am I asking questions about what I don't understand?

- Am I asking meaningful questions?
- Am I able to apply this issue or problem to my life?
- Am I applying my prior knowledge to the problem?
- Am I curious about the problem? Am I demonstrating this curiosity?
- Am I able to think imaginatively about the problem or theme?
- Am I applying reasoning skills? How am I doing this?
- Can I visualize new ideas?
- Can I apply what I have learned to other situations?
- Can I face obstacles and challenges in the learning process?
- Can I keep trying to learn, even after errors or failure?
- Can I form new questions?
- Have I taken risks? How?
- Have I been willing to work effectively alone? In groups?

Using Student Plans in the Assessment Process

Portfolio and other forms of student assessment are best used in conjunction with an explicit student plan. Minimally, this plan should specify the particular skills that the student will work on, the current level of performance, instructional methods to address these skills, and a follow-up assessment. The plan should also specify the kind of evidence that will be collected to determine the achieved level of competence.

An example of a student plan, drawn from Fingeret (1983), is provided in Exhibit 7.1. This approach to planning drawn from the Germantown Women's Educational Project, is helpful in the assessment process, as well. We include the plan here not to suggest that the specific objectives listed should necessarily be included in developmental education programs for adults. Rather, the form models an instrument and a process that can be used in all phases of the assessment process, from assessing needs and interests to documenting accomplishment of specific objectives. The form provides several categories of skills that may be of interest or relevance to adult learners in developmental education programs, including academic skills, job-related skills, and other life skills. Teachers in individual programs would need to decide which specific skills to list. From the ITB model of instruction, we would add process-related skills, such as problem solving, critical thinking, and interpersonal skills. The particular shape that the form takes is not important. Whatever the shape, the plan should include a

Exhibit 7.1.

Germantown Women's Educational Project: Learner's Goals.

Name: _____   Date: _____

Already accomplished	Goal for this session	Future goal	No interest		Evaluation and comments
				Academic	
				Work on reading:	
				Work on math:	
				Work on writing:	
				Work on: _____ (specific subject)	
				Take GED test:	
				Arts & lit.	
				Math	
				Social studies	
				Science	
				Writing	
				Prepare for trade school or college	
				Job-related	
				Learn about career options	
				Learn to fill out job application forms	
				Learn to write a resume	
				Learn to read want ads	
				Learn to type	
				Learn to use a computer	
				Improve interview skills	

Developed by the Germantown Women's Educational Project, Philadelphia, Pennsylvania.

Already accomplished	Goal for this session	Future goal	No interest		Evaluation and comments
				Family-related	
				Increase knowledge about fun/educational activities with children	
				Increase knowledge about discipline and setting limits with children	
				Increase knowledge about improving children's self-esteem	
				Increase ability to deal with school system on behalf of your children	
				Increase knowledge of family counseling resources	
				Increase knowledge of alcohol/drug abuse treatment resources	
				Increase knowledge of physical/sexual/emotional abuse resources	
				Increase knowledge of housing/utility bill resources	
				Health care	
				Obtain quality health care:	
				Dental	
				Vision	
				Gynecological	
				Prenatal	
				Learn more about women's health care issues	
				Increase ability to handle stress	

Exhibit 7.1.

Already accomplished	Goal for this session	Future goal	No interest		Evaluation and comments
				Social/community	
				Learn about candidates/political issues	
				Register to vote	
				Obtain a driver's license	
				Get a library card	
				Economic	
				Learn to budget money and organize financial records	
				Learn to open and manage a bank account	
				Learn to comparison shop and use coupons at the grocery store	
				Learn how to complete a tax return	
				Self-development	
				Keep a journal of daily thoughts/feelings	
				Learn to draw/paint/sing	
				Jog/swim/walk/aerobics	
				Plant a garden	
				Read books to relax and reduce stress	
				Take time for walks in the park/countryside	

holistic and comprehensive picture of the learner's goals and current abilities, an indication of when the goal will be worked on, progress notes, and documentation of the learner's completion of the goals.

Curricular and Instructional Assessment

Another focus of assessment in ITB instruction is to determine the effectiveness of the curricular content and materials and the teacher's instructional activities. This information can be used to make decisions about theme content and other important aspects of the learning experience. The teachers in our project use a variety of ideas to assess the effectiveness of an ITB approach to instruction, beyond a single-minded reliance on standardized test scores. We have provided their ideas in the form of a checklist (Exhibit 7.2). While not exhaustive by any means, the list may provide you with a basis for obtaining feedback on the curriculum and instructional processes you are using with your learners.

Assessing an ITB Approach in Instruction.

Teachers who are considering the ITB approach often ask themselves, "How do I know if I am doing integrated, thematic instruction?" and "How do I know if it is working?" The ABLE Network has identified ten ways to tell if the process is working:

1. Learners routinely participate in leadership and planning.
2. Learners and teachers plan and negotiate content and activities.
3. Learners routinely work with teachers, peers, and community members in the instructional experience.
4. Teachers and learners routinely reach out beyond the school for additional information.
5. Learners' life themes are integrated into instruction.
6. Learners are able to share how they solve problems, reason, and make decisions.
7. There are signs of positive collaboration among learners that continue after class.
8. Learners relate to content in personally relevant ways.
9. Learners know that correct answers may come from them as well as from the teacher.
10. Learners reflect on and assess their own learning.

Exhibit 7.2.

Checklist for Using an ITB Approach.

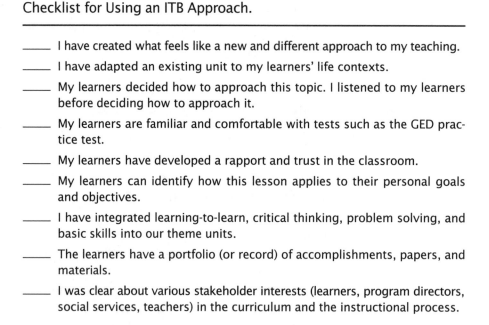

_____ I have created what feels like a new and different approach to my teaching.

_____ I have adapted an existing unit to my learners' life contexts.

_____ My learners decided how to approach this topic. I listened to my learners before deciding how to approach it.

_____ My learners are familiar and comfortable with tests such as the GED practice test.

_____ My learners have developed a rapport and trust in the classroom.

_____ My learners can identify how this lesson applies to their personal goals and objectives.

_____ I have integrated learning-to-learn, critical thinking, problem solving, and basic skills into our theme units.

_____ The learners have a portfolio (or record) of accomplishments, papers, and materials.

_____ I was clear about various stakeholder interests (learners, program directors, social services, teachers) in the curriculum and the instructional process.

One of the teachers with whom we worked named perhaps the most helpful way of gauging the success of an ITB approach. To the question "How do you know if it's working?" she quickly responded, "If my armpits are sweaty." This pithy comment clearly communicates that implementing the ITB approach is work, is risky, and can raise one's anxiety levels. Although we are certainly not recommending high levels of anxiety as a measure of success, moderate feelings of anxiousness let you know you are attending to your performance and to the effectiveness of the process. The ITB approach challenges conventional and traditional ways of planning curriculum and providing instruction. As a result, you may very well experience ambiguity, uncertainty, and even doubt. If you do, interpret these feelings as good signs, indications that you and your students have ventured into some new and exciting instructional terrain.

CHAPTER 8

Successfully Implementing ITB Instruction

Challenges and Opportunities

Successfully using an ITB approach in the education of adults involves fundamental change in the ways we think about, plan, and implement instruction. ITB instruction is grounded in distinct beliefs and assumptions about teaching and learning, the roles of the instructor and student in the learning experience, and the specific strategies and techniques used in instruction. Change is never easy in education, and moving from a traditional instructional approach toward a more ITB approach is no exception. In planning for the implementation of ITB instruction, it may be helpful to anticipate some of the challenges that might arise and to develop effective ways of addressing these challenges. These concerns are the focus of the present chapter. We will identify common challenges that have been reported in the literature and that were identified by the teachers we talked with in this project, and that came up in our own experience with the process. We will first identify the challenge and then discuss it more fully in the narrative that follows.

- *Implementing an ITB approach may require rethinking basic beliefs and assumptions that have traditionally guided and shaped education for adults.* Implicit beliefs and theories about teaching and learning significantly influence what practitioners do when working with adult learners (Dirkx & Spurgin, 1992). Therefore, when planning and implementing this approach, it is important to make these beliefs and assumptions explicit. Several of the challenges to implementing ITB instruction discussed in this chapter involve modifying beliefs and assumptions about the nature of teaching and learning.

ITB instruction is grounded in a set of beliefs and assumptions about teaching and learning that are, in some ways, different from those that characterize more traditional approaches in developmental education. Traditional instruction tends to focus on desired *outcomes* that are determined *prior* to instruction. Planning for instruction involves identifying the means considered most effective in producing these outcomes. In ITB approaches, however, practitioners place considerable emphasis on the *processes* used in the instructional experience. Instruction is viewed as having multiple outcomes and many of these outcomes cannot be identified prior to the learner's engagement in the instructional process. Traditional approaches are often teacher-centered or teacher-directed, while ITB approaches are more learner-centered. Students are more involved in planning and making decisions about their learning experiences.

While changing one's philosophy or belief systems is always difficult, the philosophical assumptions in which the ITB approach is grounded are playing an increasingly important role in organizational development and transformation of the workplace throughout the world. At the core of ITB instruction is an emphasis on democratic values and processes, on involving and engaging learners in what they are learning. Changes in the perspectives that have guided traditional education for so long will take time, and practitioners need to allow themselves and their programs sufficient time to make this transition.

It is not unusual for some institutions to take five years to implement a fully integrated approach to instruction successfully. If programs have a large enough staff, a curriculum committee should be organized to help plan and facilitate implementation of this approach. Programs should develop long-range plans for adopting ITB instruction and then implement these plans through a series of short-term goals. In smaller programs, the administrator and the program teachers may need to do this planning together.

Staff development covering the theory and practice of ITB instruction needs to be a part of this plan and will provide a common basis on which to begin rethinking beliefs and assumptions about teaching and learning. More formal staff development programs should be complemented with informal opportunities for staff to talk with each other about what they are doing, how the approach is working for them, and ways of addressing specific problems. This activity could be something as simple as a thirty- to forty-five-minute staff meeting once a week or every other week to discuss ITB instruction. Teachers will learn more from each other as they engage in the process than they will from formal staff development programs. Formal programs should be viewed merely as a catalyst for change and a source of information for program staff.

• *Administrative structures in adult developmental education, such as open entry/open exit enrollment, may need to be modified to implement ITB instruction effectively.* Organizational and administrative structures influence what goes on in teaching and learning. In developmental education programs for adults, these structures may play a greater or lesser role in shaping the nature of the instructional process. One well-known example of this relationship is the enrollment policy. Many developmental education programs for adults function with open entry/open exit enrollment. This means that individuals participating in the program may enroll or leave at any time. This policy is consistent with the highly individualistic nature of many these programs. Open entry/open exit is felt to increase access for learners and to help them take advantage of what these programs have to offer.

On its face, a managed enrollment policy would seem to limit access and reduce the opportunities for adults to learn. Managed enrollment refers to allowing individuals to start the program only within a given time frame. Individuals are then asked to commit themselves, usually in writing, to a definite period of instruction, ranging from several weeks to as long as one year. Some argue, however, that managed enrollment policies place more responsibility on learners for staying with the program and actually increase their commitment to and persistence in their learning. In addition, managed enrollment contributes to a more stable and potentially cohesive social context for learning. It allows for more work in groups that can extend beyond the limits of the instructional period. The quality of relationships that form among learners is often quite different. One group of students we observed openly referred to their group as a "family."

Clearly, within developmental education programs for adults, a tension exists between trying to provide for a high-quality learning experience and enhancing access for learners. Maintaining a completely open entry/open exit enrollment policy does little for adult learners if it makes teachers overwhelmed with numbers of students that they cannot adequately teach, or if learners come and go so frequently that little, if any, consistency or continuity is achieved within the learning environment. The success of managed enrollment depends, in part, on how potential students perceive the program. Managed enrollment has to be considered part of an overall instructional improvement process and not a distinct and separate change. When learners perceive the quality, meaning, and relevance of their learning experience to be high, managed enrollment tends to work very well. Learners value their space within the program and are less willing to lose it or give up by violating their pre-enrollment agreements with the teacher. Teachers of successful managed enrollment programs told us that limiting the experience both in terms of numbers of students and opportunities to enroll tended to enhance the value of the program to those in it. These teachers had relatively high levels of persistence and little attrition within their enrollment periods.

Those creating programs will need to determine the appropriate length of time for enrollment periods. Some factors that might influence this decision are funding sources, demand for the program's services, availability of teachers, and characteristics of the learners. We recommend that changes in enrollment policy be made gradually and conservatively. It may be best to start simply with common start times for groups. If this is not already done with the program, students can be asked to start at certain times during the month, such as every other Monday. As teachers and administrators get a feel for how this process is working, they may wish to extend the period of time between enrollments.

• *Teachers need to give themselves time to become comfortable with the different methods and processes used in ITB instruction.* Instructors in developmental programs for adults tend to be very practical. When they participate in staff development programs, they seek information and strategies to address clearly defined problems in their practice setting. Moving toward an ITB approach to instruction will be messier than teachers will expect and it may seem, for a while, that such an approach is causing more problems than it is solving.

In traditional approaches to developmental education for adults, learning settings are structured around the academic content to be mastered. While instruction may be individualized, practitioners usually rely on commercially prepared print material as a primary resource for learning. Through the use of these methods and materials, the practitioners reduce the ambiguity and uncertainty characteristic of loosely structured social situations and derive some comfort in the control inherent in these approaches.

ITB instruction is centered on the life experiences of the learners, and through problem posing and theme selection, teachers allow these experiences to drive the rest of the instructional process. Learners are heavily involved in determining their goals and structuring their learning experiences. They often plan their sessions with the teacher and take an active role in assessing their learning gains. To the outside observer, an ITB classroom can appear confusing and even somewhat chaotic. Rather than attempting to reduce uncertainty and ambiguity through more structured methods, the practitioner uses these qualities to enhance the instructional process. Students are drawn into the

Successfully Implementing ITB Instruction   **127**

learning experience in ways that encourage them to engage actively in problem solving and decision making. Rather than relying on the teacher to resolve issues for them, they learn to construct their own solutions to perceived problems with the learning setting.

Teachers who become comfortable with ITB instruction experience a shift in their perspective on the learning setting. They realize that there is little that is predictable or certain with instructional settings. They begin to see much of their practice as uncertain, ambiguous, and unpredictable. They become more responsive to the needs and issues that emerge within the learning group as its members work together. These needs and issues represent "teachable moments"—times when the group announces it is ready for a teacher. But learning to live and be comfortable with these kinds of instructional experiences will take time and a willingness to make mistakes. Through openly sharing these experiences with their students, teachers can model what it means to learn from one's experience. In ITB instruction, teachers need to become learners and let learners become their teachers.

• *To experience success and feel satisfied with ITB instruction, teachers will need training and preparation.* As indicated earlier, ITB instruction involves different philosophical assumptions, as well as different methods, techniques, and materials. Teachers implementing this approach need to feel that what they are doing is important and to be confident that they can successfully use its strategies. For this reason, teachers not experienced with this method should have staff development. Formal training sessions should be provided in four- to six-hour blocks that focus on particular aspects of the process. Teachers then need opportunities to practice what they have learned in these sessions. Practice periods should be followed by another four- to six-hour session in which the teachers can talk about and receive feedback on their work from each other and the facilitator. These follow-up sessions can be used to introduce new content and to keep expanding the teachers' skill in ITB instruction.

Ideally, rather than using traditional approaches, staff development should model the principles and process of ITB approaches. Similar to work with adult learners, teachers should help shape or influence the themes around which training will be organized. Depending on the needs and interests of the staff, themes might mirror the different chapters in this *Guide*. For example, separate training sessions could be developed for theme selection, instructional strategies, and assessment. Additional workshops may be needed on planning ITB instruction, designing and selecting appropriate instructional materials, and working with administrative staff within programs.

In this process of staff development, it is important to give teachers an opportunity in their practice settings to talk with one another and share successes and failures. As we indicated earlier, it is our belief that teachers can learn more from each other than from formal training programs. Informal staff meetings, where some time can be spent discussing ITB instruction, are one way to provide this forum. Having teachers work in teams or pairs or shadowing other teachers who may be more experienced in this approach are other methods that can foster the knowledge, skills, and beliefs necessary for using this approach effectively.

• *In light of reduced funding in many areas, program directors may need to seek creative ways to support and implement needed staff development activities.* Developmental education programs for adults in the United States have not fared well in recent budget decisions at the federal level and in many states. One of the first victims to fall to these kinds of budget cuts in education is professional and staff development. Lack of funding for staff development may make it difficult to prepare teachers adequately in this approach. Such an economic context requires those concerned with the improvement of education for adults to be resourceful in providing the professional and staff development necessary for such improvements.

One interesting and exciting approach is reflected in peer-training methods. Depending on the resources of the local program, peer training can take several different forms. One is the "train-the-trainer" model. Teachers in some programs may wish to provide extensive training to one or more experienced teachers. These teachers could, in turn, provide in-depth and continual training to their peers at the local level. Teachers from one program could spend time in another program "shadowing" peers who have more of a background with the ITB approach. Teachers who may be less experienced or knowledgeable in the methods of ITB instruction can coteach for a time with those who have had more training. They could spend one or two weeks team teaching and then work for a while on their own. Then, the less experienced teacher could return to the team situation, but this time take the lead and ask the cooperating teacher to provide feedback on her or his instructional process.

Teachers may also want to supplement these staff development activities with more self-directed methods. It may be helpful to watch training videotapes on such topics as integrating instruction, cooperative learning techniques, individual differences within the instructional process, or authentic assessment methods (e.g., student portfolios). Numerous professional development books on various aspects of ITB instruction are also available and can help teachers rethink their approach to teaching and learning. Many of these are listed in Resource B of this *Guide.*

• *The ITB approach may initially require more time to implement than traditional methods.* It is our experience that, in many settings of developmental education for adults, methods for planning and implementing instruction reflect the often severe limitations of time and materials available to practitioners. Indeed, teachers in adult basic education say that a lack of time most often impedes successful implementation of innovation in their practices (Turner & Dirkx, in press). This problem is particularly acute among programs in which staff members teach only a few hours per week, while perhaps working full-time in another job and trying to manage their family responsibilities. A lack of time to learn, master, and plan new approaches to instruction is probably the single most important reason changes have not been adopted more quickly in many of these developmental education programs.

ITB instruction will initially take more time than traditional methods. A critical principle of the ITB approach is learner involvement in the process. When learners are encouraged to participate in decision making, more time is required to help them get used to this different way of being and making decisions. Sometimes, the length of time required to identify and select themes can frustrate students as well as instructors.

Practitioners need to keep in mind, however, that decision making is itself part of the learning process in this approach and that students are engaging in important learning experiences as they participate in planning. In this phase of the instructional process, students practice many traditional academic skills, such as reading, writing, and language arts, as well as skills in problem solving, critical thinking, teamwork, interpersonal communication, and negotiation. Teachers can heighten awareness of the multilayered nature of this learning experience by periodically asking the learners to step back and reflect on what they have been doing. Teachers can guide these discussion periods by providing a list of skills that have been identified as important for adults to have, such as those identified in the SCANS report, and teachers can ask students can to point out where they are practicing these skills in the planning process. The important message here for practitioners and students is that the learning process potentially starts as soon as they begin to interact with each other and the material, regardless of the specific focus of this interaction.

Learners should also be encouraged to bring materials to the setting that they would like to use during the instructional process. In addition to fostering ownership over the process, their help in acquiring materials will reduce the time and effort teachers need to expend on ensuring that adequate supplies are present for the intended learning experiences. But teachers will still need to spend time up front to make this approach work. Programs that have traditionally paid their teachers only for face-to-face instructional time will need to consider providing planning time for their teachers. This issue reflects how specific concerns, such as providing the time needed to make the ITB approach work, are interconnected with modifying administrative structures and policies, and ultimately with fundamental beliefs and assumptions that guide the program and its practitioners. None of these challenges can be addressed in a piecemeal fashion. Rather, they must be part of a holistic approach to making the program more learner-centered and experience-based.

The extent of change that can be made within any single program will reflect the particular ways in which the program is staffed. Programs with practitioners that work 50 percent or more within the program may be able to implement this approach more quickly than programs in which staff members work very part-time. Our recommendation is that programs with very part-time staff start conservatively and begin to implement aspects of this approach as the educators acquire expertise and comfort with its use. It may work best to identify one or two areas on which the staff members want to work for six months or a year. Then, as they develop confidence in these parts of the process, they can add additional components, such as more instructional strategies or the use of authentic assessment procedures. All programs need to be guided by the belief that implementing ITB instruction appropriately will bring substantial benefits to the learners and that anything done to change the instructional process in this direction is better than doing nothing at all.

• *ITB instruction honors diversity among learners and emphasizes the need to adapt instruction to these differences.* Being responsive to differences among adult learners is a hallmark of learner-centered instruction. Within settings of adult learning, these differences are manifest in numerous ways, some of which are captured in the notion of "learning styles" (see Chapter Two). Other differences, however, reflect psychosocial, socioeconomic, and cultural characteristics that can significantly influence why, how, and what adults learn. Because of its tradition of "individualizing" instruction, developmental education for adults has implicitly attempted to respond to many of these differences. In adult basic education programs, for example, teachers will often try out a number of different strategies, methods, or materials in an attempt to find something that works for a particular student. Therefore, traditional programs seem capable of accommodating a wide range of differences among their students.

In ITB instruction, more emphasis is placed on group process and instructional strategies that involve several individuals working together on a particular task. Yet this approach is learner-centered and, as such, seeks to address the particular needs and differences of individual learners. Thus, there is a tension within this approach between the group needs and the individual needs.

Effective instructors in the ITB perspective do not perceive this situation as a conflict or feel that ITB instruction cannot adequately address differences among adult learners. Rather, they resolve this problem by holding both aspects of this seeming contradiction in consciousness. To facilitate ITB instruction effectively means to foster group formation and development *and* accommodate the particular needs of individual learners. This is accomplished, in part, through the use of group process, in which the group recognizes the individual's need as a problem that confronts the learning group as a whole.

As the group develops this perspective, its members begin to search for ways to help individual learners who may present particular differences that need to be taken into account within the learning environment. For example, say a group member is struggling to express herself in English and feels somewhat intimidated about voicing her concerns in the larger context of the learning setting. But in the small group, she is able to describe her feelings more clearly and confidently. The group can then ensure that the instructor and others in the setting hear and understand her concerns. Another student who thinks in concrete ways is helped by other members, who provide examples from their own life contexts of abstract concepts that may not make sense to this student.

In other words, it is the group itself that helps the instructor address individual differences within a cooperative learning setting. To accomplish this, however, the practitioner needs to nurture the group climate carefully. Constructively responding to differences among its members is a characteristic of a more mature learning group.

Practitioners need to be comfortable with the presence of discomfort and conflict within the group as it struggles to achieve this level of maturity. They can ensure that groups do not lose sight of differences, or gloss over them, in their attempt to get things done or to avoid confrontation. Teachers can point out unresolved issues, note students who are not actively participating, or observe other signs of running away from differences among the learners.

In one learning group, for example, discussion about a novel began to focus on the book's dark images and how these images seemed to be associated with evil within the story. At no time, however, did anyone consciously or specifically point out that one of the group's members was African American. When the facilitator wondered how this member might feel about the discussion of dark images as evil, the discussion intensified and focused for the remainder of the meeting on the group's relationship with this particular member. As a result, the group honored differences in how members of various racial or ethnic groups might interpret particular symbols or images.

Summary

In this chapter, we have identified several challenges that our participating teachers identified as particularly essential to address in planning and implementing ITB instruction. These issues underscore the importance of seeing this form of instruction not just as a new technique to use in the developmental education of adults but as a profoundly different way of thinking about this instruction. These challenges represent to us, and to many teachers who have struggled with them, *opportunities* to revisit and revise our beliefs and attitudes about instruction for adults, and the methods we use to act on these beliefs and attitudes. Rather than being insurmountable obstacles, they invite us to have new ways of thinking and being with the adult learners with whom we work. They are *our* teachers and they bring to us the teachable moment. It is up to us to make the most of it.

Academic Competencies and Life and Process Skills

This section of the Resources provides two approaches to defining competencies in which teachers of developmental education for adults may wish to ground their instruction. The first list names eight competencies that have been identified in the academic, life, and process areas, and describes more detailed characteristics to provide a sense of what is expected within these areas. The second group of competencies is more specifically related to the workplace and is derived from the ABLE Network (Adult Basic Literacy Educators Network, n.d.).

An Overview of General Competencies in Academic, Life, and Process Skills

In this section, we describe competencies for the following general skills areas: (1) basic skills; (2) thinking skills; (3) use of information; (4) interpersonal skills; (5) skill with systems; (6) skill with technology; (7) use of resources; and (8) personal qualities.

Basic Skills

Reading. The student locates, understands, and interprets written information in prose and documents—including manuals, graphs, and schedules—to perform tasks; learns from a text by determining the main idea or essential message; identifies relevant details, facts, and specifications; infers or locates the meaning of unknown or technical vocabulary; and judges the accuracy, appropriateness, style, and plausibility of reports, proposals, or theories of other writers.

Writing.   A student communicates thoughts, ideas, information, and messages in writing; records information completely and accurately; composes and creates documents, such as letters, directions, manuals, reports, proposals, graphs, flow charts; and uses language, style, organization, and format appropriate to the subject matter, purpose, and audience. In a written piece, the student includes supporting documentation; attends to detail; and checks, edits, and revises for correct information, appropriate emphasis, form, grammar, spelling, and punctuation.

Arithmetic.   The student performs basic computations; uses basic numerical concepts such as whole numbers and percentages in practical situations; makes reasonable estimates of arithmetic results without a calculator; and uses tables, graphs, diagrams, and charts to obtain or convey quantitative information.

Mathematics.   The student approaches practical problems by choosing appropriately from a variety of mathematical techniques; uses quantitative data to construct logical explanations for real-world situations; expresses mathematical ideas and concepts orally and in writing; and understands the role of chance in the occurrence and prediction of events.

Listening.   The student receives, attends to, interprets, and responds to verbal messages and other cues such as body language in ways that are appropriate to the purpose; for example, to comprehend, learn, evaluate critically, appreciate, or support the speaker.

Speaking.   The student organizes ideas and communicates oral messages appropriate to listeners and situations; participates in conversations, discussions, and group presentations; selects an appropriate medium for conveying a message; uses verbal language and other cues such as body language appropriate in style, tone, and level of complexity to the audience and occasion; speaks clearly and communicates a message; understands and responds to listener feedback; and asks questions when needed.

Thinking Skills

Creative Thinking. The student uses imagination freely, combines ideas or information in new ways, makes connections between seemingly unrelated ideas, and reshapes goals in ways that reveal new possibilities.

Decision Making. The student specifies goals and constraints, generates alternatives, considers risks, and evaluates and chooses best alternatives.

Problem Solving. The student recognizes that a problem exists (i.e., there is a discrepancy between what is and what should or could be), identifies possible reasons for the discrepancy, and devises a plan of action to resolve it. He or she evaluates and monitors progress and revises the plan as indicated by findings.

Seeing Things in the Mind's Eye. The student organizes and processes symbols, pictures, graphs, objects or other information. For example, he or she can imagine a building from a blueprint, a system's operation from schematics, the flow of work activities from narrative descriptions, or the taste of food from reading a recipe.

Knowing How to Learn. The student recognizes and can use learning techniques to apply and adapt new knowledge and skills in both familiar and changing situations. The student is aware of learning tools, such as personal learning styles (visual, aural, etc.), formal learning strategies (note taking or clustering items that share some characteristics), and informal learning strategies (awareness of unidentified false assumptions that may lead to faulty conclusions).

Reasoning. The student discovers a rule or principle underlying the relationship between two or more objects and applies it in solving a problem. For example, he or she uses logic to draw conclusions from available information; extracts rules or principles from a set of objects or written text; applies rules and principles to a new situation; or determines which conclusions are correct when given a set of facts and a set of conclusions.

Use of Information

Acquiring and Evaluating Information. The student identifies need for data, obtains data from existing sources or creates them, and evaluates their relevance and accuracy.

Organizing and Maintaining Information. The student organizes, processes, and maintains written or computerized records and other forms of information in a systematic fashion.

Interpreting and Communicating Information. The student selects and analyzes information and communicates the results to others using oral, written, graphic, pictorial, or multimedia methods.

Using Computers to Process Information. The student employs computers to acquire, organize, analyze, and communicate information.

Interpersonal Skills

Participating as a Member of a Team. The student works cooperatively with others and contributes to the group with ideas, suggestions, and effort.

Teaching Others. The student helps others learn, is giving of self, and has the clarity needed to understand others' confusion.

Serving Clients or Customers. The student works and communicates with clients or customers to satisfy their expectations.

Exercising Leadership. The student communicates thoughts, feelings, and ideas to justify a position; encourages, persuades, convinces, or otherwise motivates an individual or groups; and responsibly challenges existing procedures, policies, or authority.

Negotiating. The student works toward an agreement that may involve exchanging specific resources or resolving divergent interests.

Working with Cultural Diversity. The student works well with men and women and with people from a variety of ethnic, social, or educational backgrounds.

Skill with Systems

Understanding Systems. The student knows how social, organizational, and technological systems work and operates effectively within them.

Monitoring and Correcting Performance. The student distinguishes trends, predicts the impact of actions on system operations, diagnoses deviations in the function of a system or organization, and takes necessary action to correct performance.

Improving and Designing Systems. The student suggests ways to modify existing systems to improve products or services and develops new or alternative systems.

Skill with Technology

Selecting Technology. The student judges which set of procedures, tools, or machines, including computers and their programs, will produce the desired results.

Applying Technology to Task. The student understands the overall intent and proper procedures for setting up and operating machines, including computers and their programming systems.

Maintaining and Troubleshooting Technology. The student prevents, identifies, or solves problems in machines, computers, and other technologies.

Use of Resources

Allocating Time. The student selects relevant, goal-related activities; ranks them in order of importance; allocates time to activities; and understands, prepares, and follows schedules.

Allocating Money. The student uses or prepares budgets, including making cost and revenue forecasts; keeps detailed records to track budget performance; and makes appropriate adjustments.

Allocating Material and Facility Resources. The student acquires, stores, and distributes materials, supplies, parts, equipment, space, or final products in order to make the best use of them.

Allocating Human Resources. The student assesses knowledge and skills, distributes work accordingly, evaluates performance, and provides feedback.

Personal Qualities

Responsibility. The student exerts a high level of effort and perseverance toward attaining goals; works hard to excel at tasks by setting high standards, paying attention to details, working well, and displaying a high level of concentration even when assigned an unpleasant task; and displays high standards of attendance, punctuality, enthusiasm, vitality, and optimism in approaching and completing tasks.

Self-Esteem.   The student believes in own self-worth and maintains a positive view of self; demonstrates knowledge of own skills and abilities; is aware of impact on others; and knows own emotional capacity and needs and how to address them.

Sociability.   The student demonstrates understanding, friendliness, adaptability, empathy, and politeness in new and ongoing group settings; asserts self in familiar and unfamiliar social situations; relates well to others; responds appropriately as the situation requires; and takes an interest in what others say and do.

Self-Management.   The student assesses own knowledge, skills, and abilities accurately; sets well-defined and realistic personal goals; monitors progress toward goal attainment and motivates self through goal achievement; exhibits self-control; responds to feedback unemotionally and undefensively; and is a self-starter.

Integrity and Honesty.   The student can be trusted. He or she recognizes a decision or behavior that may break with commonly held personal or societal values; understands how violating these beliefs and codes affects an organization, self, and others; and chooses an ethical course of action.

Skills List from the ABLE Network

The ABLE Network has defined specific competencies related to the workplace. The categories of skills are learning-to-learn, thinking, personal management for the job, influence, math, and reading. The specific characteristics for these skills are listed below each category. This skills list appears in Exhibit A.1.

Exhibit A.1.
Skills List from the ABLE Network.

Learning to Learn (L)

Personal (P)
LP 1   Identify how they learn most easily (preferred learning style)
LP 2   Accommodate their styles to different environments
LP 3   Organize their time and materials

Interpersonal (I)
LI 1   Give and receive feedback appropriately
LI 2   Learn from and with other people

Cognitive (C)
LC 1   Organize information
LC 2   Relate, recall, and apply information
LC 3   Think convergently (focus) and divergently (brainstorm)
LC 4   Use critical, creative, and intuitive evaluation skills
LC 5   Find and use expert, peer, and written resources

Thinking Skills (T)

Problem-solving skills (P)
TP 1   Identify problems
TP 2   Generate ideas about the causes(s) of a problem
TP 3   Identify the cause of a problem
TP 4   Identify solutions to the problem
TP 5   Choose appropriate solutions(s)
TP 6   Apply appropriate solution
TP 7   Evaluate the solution
TP 8   Modify the solution, as needed

Higher-order thinking skills (H)
TH 1   Analyze the components of a process, procedure, or system
TH 2   Compare the effectiveness of at least two processes, procedures, or systems
TH 3   Draw conclusions or make predictions about a process, procedure, or system
TH 4   Evaluate the effectiveness or efficiency of a process, procedure, system, or decision

Creative thinking skills (C)
TC 1   Generate new solutions to common conditions or problems
TC 2   Organize and process diverse kinds of information in meaningful ways

Personal management for the job (P)

Self-Esteem (S)
PS 1   Understand how one's self-esteem affects performance
PS 2   Learn from one's mistakes
PS 3   Accept appropriate criticism and praise
PS 4   State personal needs clearly and assertively
PS 5   Channel emotional reactions constructively
PS 6   Take appropriate risks

Goal setting/Motivation (G)
PG 1   Identify personal and work values
PG 2   Identify attainable and realistic long-term needs that motivate personal growth

Personal development (P)
PP 1   Use employment-related forms, i.e., applications for social security, W-4s
PP 2   Prepare job applications, resumes, and letters of application
PP 3   Identify and use appropriate sources of information about job opportunities
PP 4   Prepare for and participate in a job interview

Negotiation (N)
GN 1   Understand the concept of conflict and use strategies for handling it
GN 2   Understand the benefits of negotiation and when to use it
GN 3   Negotiate an issue

Teamwork (T)
GT 1   Understand the concept of teamwork, courtesy, and cooperation
GT 2   Identify and assess their roles in a team and norms or rules of behavior that contribute to a team's effectiveness
GT 3   Identify issues around team leadership, including leader and follower styles
GT 4   Be an effective and flexible team member
GT 5   Understand different work environments and their effects on teams
GT 6   Demonstrate effective interteam communication

Influence (I)

Organizational effectiveness (O)
IO 1   Interpret written and unwritten values and goals of various types of organizations
IO 2   Determine the compatibility of their personal and organizational values

Career growth within an organization (C)
IC 1   Recognize requirements for career advancement
IC 2   Recognize how their behaviors affect their job performance and satisfaction

Leadership (L)
IL 1   Understand the difference between management and leadership
IL 2   Identify the qualities of a successful leader
IL 3   Assess own leadership skills and identify areas for improvement

Math (M)
M 1   Use money, banking, and financial services, i.e., recognize denominations of money, make change, balance a checkbook, interpret savings accounts, purchase goods and services with credit, calculate interest

M 2   Interpret budgets, bills, and income, i.e., interpret wages, wage deductions and benefits, calculate costs of child care, plan for major purchases, and demonstrate the use of a budget

M 3   Apply principles of comparison shopping in the selection of goods and services, i.e., calculate discounts, compute unit pricing, calculate sales tax, and interpret tax tables

M 4   Interpret and generate tables, charts, and graphs, i.e., height and weight tables, newspaper graphics (circle, line, and bar graphs), progress in class, household expenses and/or chores, income tax tables, information on a matrix

M 5   Determine transportation costs and interpret schedules and tables; calculate distance, rate, and time; and calculate mileage and fuel consumption

M 6   Use weights, measures, and measurement scales, i.e., interpret temperatures; calculate with units of time; interpret standard measurements for length, width, perimeter, area, volume, height and weight; and interpret product container weight and volume

Reading (R)

R 1   Look up information

R 2   Read and interpret signs, symbols, and labels

R 3   Interpret information on forms and applications

R 4   Read and interpret basic financial and legal documents, i.e., pay stub, union contract, health benefit package

R 5   Follow written instructions

R 6   Read and interpret memos and policy/procedural manuals

R 7   Interpret visual materials, i.e., diagrams, illustrations, tables, charts, and graphs

Source: From the Adult Basic Literacy Educators Network, n.d., Seattle, WA. Reprinted with permission from the *I*CANS* Project, Washington State Board for Community & Technical Colleges.

Curricular and Instructional Resources for Implementing ITB Instruction

Over the last ten years, many individuals and groups have produced written and audiovisual materials that can assist in the transition to a more integrated, thematic approach to instruction. While some of these works have come from individuals interested in furthering our scholarly understanding of this approach to instruction, others are by practitioners working in particular settings of adult developmental education who intend these works to be practical resources for other educators. In Resource B, we have compiled a modest list of those resources with which we are familiar and those we have used in our own work. Undoubtedly, the list could be greatly expanded by others working in this area.

We have organized our list into the following categories: (1) text resources for teaching and learning, (2) curricula and curriculum guides, and (3) audiovisual resources.

Text Resources for Teaching and Learning

The following materials may help provide an overall understanding of the principles at the foundations of an ITB approach. While some of these are rather theoretical, others are geared specifically to practitioners' needs and are written by practitioners working within this framework. Educators interested in deepening their understanding of contextual learning and thematic approaches to teaching adult learners will find these references helpful.

Arnold, R., & Brandt, B. (1985). *A new weave: Popular education in Canada and Central America.* Toronto: CUSO and Ontario Institute for Studies in Education.

Auerbach, E. R. (1989). Toward a social-contextual approach to family literacy. *Harvard Educational Review, 59,* 165–181.

Beder, H., et al. (1992). *Project Rise: Workplace literacy education in context.* New Brunswick, NJ: Rutgers University, Graduate School of Education.

Brady, M. (1989). *What's worth teaching? Selecting, organizing, and integrating knowledge.* Albany: State University of New York Press.

Brookfield, S. A. (1986). *Understanding and facilitating adult learning.* San Francisco: Jossey-Bass.

City University of New York. (1993). *Contextualized learning technical assistance project: Final report and handbook on contextualized learning.* New York: New York State Education Department.

Drake, S. M. (1993). *Planning integrated curriculum: The call to adventure.* Alexandria, VA: Association for Supervision and Curriculum Development.

Gordon, D. (1991). *We are all family: A multicultural basic education manual for family learning.* Philadelphia, PA: LSH Women's Program.

Gutloff, K. (Ed.). (1996). *Integrated thematic teaching.* West Haven, CT: National Education Association Professional Library.

Hart-Landsberg, S., & Reder, S. (1993). *Teamwork and literacy: Learning from a skills-poor position.* (Tech. Rep. No. TR93–6). Philadelphia, PA: National Center on Adult Literacy.

Holt, D. D. (1993). *Cooperative learning: A response to linguistic and cultural diversity.* Washington, DC: Center for Applied Linguistics.

Hope, A., & Timmel, S. (1984). *Training for transformation: A handbook for community workers* (Vols. 1–3). Gweru, Zimbabwe: Mambo Press.

Kovalik, S. (1993). *ITI the model: Integrated thematic instruction.* Village of Oak Creek, AZ: Books for Educators.

Leistyna, P., Woodrum, A., & Sherblom, S. A. (1996). *Breaking free: The transformative power of critical pedagogy.* Cambridge, MA: Harvard Educational Review.

Miller, J. P. (1988). *The holistic curriculum.* Toronto: Ontario Institute for Studies in Education Press.

Ministry of Education. (1992). *First nations studies: Curriculum assessment framework.* Victoria, BC: Author.

Shor, I. (1987). *Freire for the classroom.* Portsmouth, NH: Boynton/Cook, Heinemann.

Shor, I. (1992). *Empowering education: Critical teaching for social change.* Chicago: University of Chicago Press.

Vella, J. (1994). *Learning to listen, learning to teach: The power of dialogue in educating adults.* San Francisco: Jossey-Bass.

Wallerstein, N. C. (1983). *Language and culture in conflict: Problem-posing in the ESL classroom.* Reading, MA: Addison-Wesley.

Curricula and Curriculum Guides

A number of adult developmental education programs have developed curriculum guides or curricula that reflect the perspective taken in this book. While some are designed specifically for workplace settings, others are oriented to work within communities or with families. A few of the works listed here focus specifically on designing and implementing instructional methods, such as cooperative learning, for use in ITB instruction. These works provide useful ideas about how to develop and use ITB instruction within specific contexts of teaching and learning.

Adult Basic Literacy Educators Network. (n.d.) *I*CANS: Integrated curriculum for achieving necessary skills.* Seattle, WA: Author.

Auerbach, E. R. (1992). *Making meaning, making change: Participatory curriculum development for adult ESL literacy.* Washington DC: Center for Applied Linguistics.

Chase, N. D. (1990). *The hospital job skills enhancement program: A workplace literacy project curriculum manual.* Atlanta: Georgia State University, Center for the Study of Adult Literacy, and Grady Memorial Hospital.

Collette, M., Weaver, B., Bingman, M. B., & Merrifield, J. (1992). *Getting there: A curriculum guide for rural jobs participants.* Knoxville, TN: The Center for Literacy Studies.

Imel, S., Kerka, S., & Pritz, S. (1994). *More than the sum of the parts: Using small group learning in adult basic and literacy education.* Columbus, OH: The Ohio State University, College of Education, Center on Education and Training for Employment.

Lane Community College (1991). *Oregon state staff development cooperative learning training manual.* Salem, OR: Oregon Department of Education.

Lindsay, J. W. (1993). *You can help pregnant and parenting teens: Curriculum guide teens parenting series.* Buena Park, CA: Morning Glory Press.

Ministry of Advanced Education and Job Training. (1987). *Adult basic education/Adult basic literacy curriculum guide and resource book.* Victoria, BC: Author.

Nash, A. (1992). *Talking shop: A curriculum sourcebook for participatory adult ESL.* Washington, DC: Center for Applied Linguistics.

Schneider, M., & Clarke, M. (1995). *Dimensions of change: An authentic assessment guidebook.* Seattle, WA: Adult Basic Literacy Educators Network.

Audiovisual Resources

Instructional videotapes on the principles and practices of integrated curriculum can also be helpful tools in the professional development of educators and program administrators. We have listed a few that we have used in our work.

Achieving integration through curriculum development. Berkeley, CA: University of California, National Center for Research on Vocational Education.

Integrated, thematic curriculum: Teacher training institute. Lincoln, NE: University of Nebraska, Nebraska Institute for the Study of Adult Literacy.

Integrating academic and vocational studies. Berkeley, CA: University of California, National Center for Research on Vocational Education.

Laying the foundation for integration. Berkeley, CA: University of California, National Center for Research on Vocational Education.

Personal Notes and
Reflections for Teachers

In our work as educators, we are guided by knowledge that is both explicit and implicit. Some of what we do in our interactions with learners is known to us. As we act, we are aware of certain beliefs, values, and assumptions on which our actions are based. For example, neither one of us devotes much time in our teaching to extensive periods of lecturing and information giving, because we have a set of beliefs and values about how adults learn and the overall aims of adult learning. In acting on these beliefs, we also make certain assumptions about what activities are effective and worthwhile in furthering adult learning. We both use small groups extensively in our teaching and our interactions with these groups are influenced by what we know and believe about effective facilitation.

Yet as Donald Schön teaches us in his book *The Reflective Practitioner* (1983), we know more than we can say. Much of our work is grounded in a kind of knowing-in-action, in which we operate from a deep-seated set of core beliefs and values with little conscious awareness of the knowledge on which our actions are based. If something goes awry within our practice setting, we seldom turn to these core beliefs as a possible source of the problem. Rather, we search for new and better ways to act on those core assumptions. If one of us experiences difficulty in using small groups to further the aims of adult learners, we may not question our undying belief in the small group as a pedagogical strategy. Rather, we look for ways in which we might have inappropriately used the strategy or new techniques to overcome the difficulties that have arisen.

Some improvements in educational practice, however, depend

not on new and more effective techniques, but on educators' examining and changing some of their deep-seated beliefs—the core knowledge. Successful adoption of an ITB approach to instruction represents this kind of change. This approach to instruction challenges traditional assumptions about the aims of education, what constitutes knowledge, how adults learn and acquire knowledge, and the methods most appropriate for helping them learn. Initially, the ITB approach will raise more questions in your practice than it answers. It will invite you into a dialogue with your practice.

One way to facilitate this dialogue is through maintaining a reflective journal on your teaching. We encourage you to develop and use a journal to continue the dialogue that this process will initiate. For those of you not used to maintaining a practice journal, Resource C is a place for you to begin. We provide three exhibits in this resource. In Exhibit C.1, we invite you to reflect on your own goals for instruction within the particular practice setting in which you work. In Exhibit C.2, we encourage you to think about your learners—what you know about them, how you know what you know, and what you believe about them as individuals and learners. In Exhibit C.3, we provide a space for you to think through the steps you can use in implementing ITB instruction within your program.

Exhibit C.1.
Personal Instructional Goals.

What are my goals for this program, session, or class?

_____

_____

_____

_____

_____

_____

Are my goals for some students different than for other students? In what ways? Why are they different?

_____

_____

_____

_____

_____

_____

What instructional goals do I have for the upcoming year?

_____

_____

_____

_____

_____

_____

Exhibit C.2.

Beliefs About My Learners.

What do I know about my learners? Who are they and what they are like?

_____

_____

_____

_____

_____

_____

How do I know this about them? What are the sources of my information?

_____

_____

_____

_____

_____

_____

What do I believe about my learners and about their aims, desires, and motivations for learning?

_____

_____

_____

_____

_____

_____

Exhibit C.3.
Steps for Implementing ITB Instruction in My Program.

1. _____
   _____
2. _____
   _____
3. _____
   _____
4. _____
   _____
5. _____
   _____
6. _____
   _____
7. _____
   _____
8. _____
   _____
9. _____
   _____
10. _____
   _____
11. _____
   _____
12. _____
   _____
13. _____
   _____
14. _____
   _____
15. _____
   _____
16. _____
   _____
17. _____
   _____
18. _____
   _____
19. _____
   _____

REFERENCES

Adult Basic Literacy Educators Network. (n.d.) *I*CANS: Integrated curriculum for achieving necessary skills.* Seattle, WA: Author.

Angelo, T. A., & Cross, K. P. (1993). *Classroom assessment techniques: A handbook for college teachers.* San Francisco: Jossey-Bass.

Association for Supervision and Curriculum Development (ASCD). (1991). Integrating the curriculum. *Educational Leadership, 49,* 21–95.

Auerbach, E. R. (1989). Toward a social-contextual approach to family literacy. *Harvard Educational Review, 59,* 165–181.

Auerbach, E. R. (1992). *Making meaning, making change: Participatory curriculum development for adult ESL literacy.* Washington, DC: Center for Applied Linguistics.

Auerbach, E. R., & Wallerstein, N. (1987). *ESL for action: Problem-posing at work.* Teachers' guide. Reading, MA: Addison-Wesley.

Bonwell, C. C., & Eison, J. A. (1991). *Active learning: Creating excitement in the classroom* (ASHE-ERIC Higher Education Report No. 1). Washington, DC: George Washington University, School of Education and Human Development.

Brady, M. (1986). Models for curriculum development: The theory and practice. *Curriculum and Teaching, 1,* 25–32.

Brady, M. (1989). *What's worth teaching? Selecting, organizing, and integrating knowledge.* Albany: State University of New York Press.

Brandt, R. (1991). On interdisciplinary curriculum: A conversation with Heidi Hayes Jacobs. *Educational Leadership, 49,* 24–26.

Brookfield, S. A. (1986). *Understanding and facilitating adult learning.* San Francisco: Jossey-Bass.

Brophy, J., & Alleman, J. (1991). A caveat: Curriculum integration isn't always a good idea. *Educational Leadership, 49,* 66.

Carnevale, A. P., Gainer, L. J., & Meltzer, A. S. (1988). *Workplace basics: The skills employers want.* Washington, DC: U.S. Department of Labor and the American Society for Training and Development.

Chase, N. D. (1990). *The hospital job skills enhancement program: A workplace literacy project curriculum manual.* Atlanta: Georgia State University, Center for the Study of Adult Literacy, and Grady Memorial Hospital.

Cranton, P. (1994). *Understanding and promoting transformative learning: A guide for educators of adults.* San Francisco: Jossey-Bass.

Cranton, P. (1996). *Professional development as transformative learning: New perspective for teachers of adults.* San Francisco: Jossey-Bass.

Dale, E. (1954). *Audiovisual methods in teaching.* New York: Dryden Press.

Daloz, L. A. (1986). *Effective teaching and mentoring: Realizing the transformational power of adult learning experiences.* San Francisco: Jossey-Bass.

Dirkx, J. M. (1995). *Evaluation of adult basic education programs: Final report.* Lincoln, NE: University of Nebraska, Nebraska Institute for the Study of Adult Literacy.

Dirkx, J. M., & Crawford, M. (1993). Teaching reading through teaching science: Development and evaluation of an experimental curriculum for correctional ABE programs. *The Journal of Correctional Education, 44,* 172–176.

Dirkx, J. M., & Jha, L. R. (1994). Predicting rapid completion, persistence, and attrition in adult basic education. *Adult Education Quarterly, 45,* 269–285.

Dirkx, J. M., & Spurgin, M. (1992). Implicit theories of adult basic education teachers: How they think about their students. *Adult Basic Education: An Interdisciplinary Journal for Adult Literacy Educators, 2,* 20–41.

Drake, S. M. (1993). *Planning integrated curriculum: The call to adventure.* Alexandria, VA: Association for Supervision and Curriculum Development.

Ennis, R. (1991). Learning in small adult literacy groups. *Australian Journal of Adult and Community Education, 30,* 105–110.

Fingeret, A. (1983). Social network: A new perspective on independence and illiterate adults. *Adult Education Quarterly, 33,* 133–146.

Fingeret, H. A. (1990). Who are illiterate adults? *Adult Learning, 1*(6), 27.

Fogarty, R. (1991). Ten ways to integrate curriculum. *Educational Leadership, 49,* 61–65.

Fogarty, R. (1992). Ways to integrate curriculum. *The Education Digest, 57,* 53–57.

Freire, P. (1970). *Pedagogy of the oppressed.* New York: Seabury Press.

Gardner, H. (1983). *Frames of mind: The theory of multiple intelligences.* New York: Basic Books.

Goodsell, A., Maher, M., & Tinto, V. (1992). *Collaborative learning: A sourcebook for higher education.* University Park, PA: National Center on Postsecondary Teaching, Learning, and Assessment.

Gutloff, K. (Ed.). (1996). *Integrated thematic teaching.* West Haven, CT: National Education Association Professional Library.

Hart-Landsberg, S., & Reder, S. (1993). *Teamwork and literacy: Learning from a skills-poor position.* (Tech. Rep. No. TR93–6). Philadelphia, PA: National Center on Adult Literacy.

Hope, A., & Timmel, S. (1984). *Training for transformation: A handbook for community workers* (Vols. 1–3). Gweru, Zimbabwe: Mambo Press.

Imel, S., Kerka, S., & Pritz, S. (1994). *More than the sum of the parts: Using small group learning in adult basic and literacy education.* Columbus, OH: The Ohio State University, College of Education, Center on Education and Training for Employment.

Jacobs, H. H. (Ed.). (1989). *Interdisciplinary curriculum: Design and implementation.* Alexandria, VA : Association for Supervision and Curriculum Development.

Jacobs, H. H. (1991). Planning for curriculum integration. *Educational Leadership, 49,* 27–28.

Jarvis, P. (1992). *Paradoxes of learning: Becoming an individual in society.* San Francisco: Jossey-Bass.

Jones, R. M. (1968). *Fantasy and feeling in education.* New York: Harper & Row.

Kagan, S. (1989, December). The structural approach to cooperative learning. *Educational Leadership, 47*(4), 12–15.

Kirkness, V. (1982). Workshop ideas for mini think-ins. In V. Friesen, J. Archibald, & R. Jack (Eds.), *Creating cultural awareness about first nations.* Vancouver, BC: University of British Columbia.

Kolb, D. A. (1984). *Experiential learning.* Englewood Cliffs, NJ: Prentice Hall.

Kovalik, S. (1993). *ITI the model: Integrated thematic instruction.* Village of Oak Creek, AZ: Books for Educators.

Lane Community College. (1991). *Oregon state staff development cooperative learning training manual.* Salem, OR: Oregon Department of Education.

McLaughlin, P. (1993). *Interacting with others: An affective skills curriculum.* Seattle, WA: Adult Basic Literacy Educators (ABLE) Network.

Merriam, S. B., & Caffarella, R. S. (1991). *Learning in adulthood: A comprehensive guide.* San Francisco: Jossey-Bass.

Ministry of Advanced Education and Job Training. (1987). *Adult basic education/Adult basic literacy curriculum guide and resource book.* Victoria, BC: Author.

Nickse, R. S. (1990). *Family and intergenerational literacy programs: An update of "The noises of literacy"* (Information Series, No. 342). Columbus, OH: ERIC Clearinghouse on Adult, Career, & Vocational Education. (ERIC Document Reproduction Service No. ED 327 736)

Pratt, D. D. (1988). Andragogy as a relational construct. *Adult Education Quarterly, 38,* 160–181.

Prawat, R. S. (1991). The value of ideas: The immersion approach to the development of thinking. *Educational Researcher, 20,* 3–10, 30.

Presseisen, B. Z., Sternberg, R. J., Fischer, K. W., Knight, C. C., & Feuerstein, R. (1990). *Learning and thinking styles: Classroom interaction.* Washington, DC: National Education Association.

Quigley, B. A. (1990). Hidden logic: Reproduction and resistance in adult literacy and adult basic education. *Adult Education Quarterly, 40,* 103–115.

Quigley, B. A. (1992). The disappearing student: The attrition problem in adult basic education. *Adult Learning, 31,* 25–26.

Quigley, B. A. (1997). *Rethinking literacy education: The critical need for practice-based change.* San Francisco: Jossey-Bass.

Quigley, B. A., & Holsinger, E. (1993). "Happy consciousness": Ideology and hidden curricula in literacy education. *Adult Education Quarterly, 44,* 17–33.

Reiff, J. C. (1992). *Learning styles.* Washington, DC: National Education Association.

Rogoff, B., & Lave, J. (1984). *Everyday cognition and its development in social context.* Cambridge, MA: Harvard University Press.

Sarmiento, A. R., & Kay, A. (1990). *Worker-centered learning: A union guide to workplace literacy.* Washington, DC: AFL-CIO Human Resources Development Institute.

SCANS. (1991). What work requires of schools: A SCANS report for America 2000. Washington, DC: Department of Labor, Secretary's Commission on Achieving Necessary Skills. (ERIC Document Reproduction Service No. ED 332 054)

Schneider, M., & Clarke, M. (1995). *Dimensions of change: An authentic assessment guidebook.* Seattle, WA: Adult Basic Literacy Educators Network.

Schön, D. (1983). *The reflective practitioner: How professionals think in action.* New York: Basic Books.

Schwartz, R. M. (1994). *The skilled facilitator: Practical wisdom for developing effective groups.* San Francisco: Jossey-Bass.

Shor, I. (1992). *Empowering education: Critical teaching for social change.* Chicago: University of Chicago Press.

Soifer, R., Irwin, M. E., Crumrine, B. M., Honzaki, E., Simmons, B. K., & Young, D. L. (1990). *The complete theory-to-practice handbook of adult literacy: Curriculum design and teaching approaches.* New York: Teachers College Press.

Sticht, T. G. (1991). *Functional context education: Learning for and in the world of work.* El Cajon, CA: U.S. Department of Education.

Turner, M. K., & Dirkx, J. M. (in press). Beyond the vessel: Fostering adoption of innovation and change in adult education practice. *Adult Basic Education: An Interdisciplinary Journal for Adult Literacy Educators.*

Vars, G. F. (1991). Integrated curriculum in historical perspective. *Educational Leadership, 49,* 14–15.

Vella, J. (1994). *Learning to listen, learning to teach: The power of dialogue in educating adults.* San Francisco: Jossey-Bass.

Young, M. B., Fleischman, H., Fitzgerald, N., & Morgan, M. A. (1995). *National evaluation of adult education programs: Executive summary.* Arlington, VA: Development Associates.

Zacharakis-Jutz, J., & Dirkx, J. M. (1993). Unresolved issues in state and federally funded workplace literacy programs: Toward a rational perspective and policy. *Adult Basic Education: An Interdisciplinary Journal for Adult Literacy Educators, 3,* 91–105.

INDEX